**Martyn Brunt** writes a monthly column for *220 Triathlon* magazine. His obsession led him to sell his Mercedes, give away his expensive suit, chuck in his City job and become, in his father's words, a 'god-damned hippy' (a cycle path designer with a camper van).

D1322370

# Accidental Ironman

Martyn Brunt

Constable • London

Constable & Robinson Ltd.
55–56 Russell Square
London WC1B 4HP
www.constablerobinson.com

First published in the UK by Constable,
an imprint of Constable & Robinson Ltd., 2013

Copyright © Martyn Brunt, 2013

The right of Martyn Brunt to be identified as the author of this
work has been asserted by him in accordance with the
Copyright, Designs & Patents Act 1988

All rights reserved. This book is sold subject to the condition
that it shall not, by trade or otherwise, be lent, re-sold,
hired out or otherwise circulated in any form of binding or cover
other than that in which it is published and without a similar condition
including this condition being imposed on a subsequent purchaser.

A copy of the British Library Cataloguing in
Publication Data is available from the British Library

ISBN: 978-1-47211-105-0 (paperback)
ISBN: 978-1-47211-109-8 (ebook)

Printed and bound by
CPI Group (UK) Ltd, Croydon, CR0 4YY

10 9 8 7 6 5 4 3 2 1

# Chapter 1

I am standing waist deep in the waters of the Main Donnau Canal near Nuremberg in Germany. I am clad in a neoprene wetsuit, swim hat and goggles, and my face bears the slightly distracted look of someone with an undiagnosed urinary tract infection. As I stare blankly into the middle distance, like a man modelling pants in a catalogue, I am dimly aware that standing around me are people dressed exactly the same way as me – hundreds of them. However, the presence of what looks like the entire cast of *March of the Penguins* around me is not a cause for joy, because with several hundred swimmers all about to set off at the same time in the same narrow stretch of water, there's a high chance I'll get their *Happy Feet* in my face. My nerves, coupled with having water lapping around my clinkers, have caused me to leak a small amount of wee down my leg, which makes me think:

1.  I wonder how many other dirty bastards have done the same, and

2.  That actually feels quite nice

Suddenly there is a loud bang, which I assume is the sound of my arse caving in but is, in fact, the start cannon for the 'wave' in front of ours. There are so many swimmers in the canal that we are setting off in waves of a few hundred at a time – and mine is next. If you're reading this in the UK, you're probably wondering how you fit hundreds of swimmers into a strip of water about as wide as Peter Crouch lengthways, but here in Germany they do things properly and the Main Donnau Canal is wide enough to take ships and, possibly, Peter Crouch sideways. Some of us are standing near the edge on the sloping bank so as not to expend energy treading water and, frankly, drink other people's piss. Others are bobbing about in the water trying to keep their mouths shut, while others stay sitting on the bank silently listening to the power ballads being pumped out of the massive speakers attached to the bridge behind us. Somewhat stereotypically it sounds a lot like David Hasselhoff, although I am wearing a swim cap and my ears are full of water, which probably makes everything sound like Der Hoff.

It is now our turn to move forward to the start line, and those of us near the bank glide silently into the water to begin the bunfight for start positions. Thousands of spectators standing on the banks and the bridge cheer as we adopt hard, flinty expressions on our faces in a bid to look windswept and interesting. Starting positions matter, so there is some jockeying to be done. If, like me, you swim front crawl by breathing only to the right-hand side, you want to be on the left-hand side of the starting area so you can see all the buggers around you and reduce the chances of getting clumped about the head by someone swimming on your 'blind' side. If, like me, you are a 'reasonable' swimmer then you want to be NEAR to the front of the wave so you avoid all the doggy-paddlers, hand-slashers and panickers, but you don't want to be AT the front where the piranha pack lurks, ready to swim over the top of you and make you feel as though you've just emerged from a washing machine. I have carefully selected my favoured position and set about preventing anyone else coming within five feet of it by treading water and surreptitiously booting anyone who comes too close – as well as studying those around me in a bid to clairvoyantly judge their swimming abilities, because you always get some dickhead who puts themselves at the front, sets off like a rocket and then dies on their arse after 200 metres.

Swimming fast for 200m is no good in our present circumstances because ahead of us lies a swim of 3.8 kilometres. Actually, what really lies ahead of us is 140.6 miles of racing in what is arguably the hardest mainstream sport in the world. Now that you've reached this page in the book I'm going to assume you're not one of those people who is reading this while standing in WHSmith like it's some kind of fucking lending library, and I feel safe revealing to you what I'm doing bobbing about in the waters of the Main Donnau Canal. The event that has drawn me here is called an Ironman, an endurance triathlon event made up of a 3.8-kilometre swim, a 112-mile cycle (sorry for jumping between distance measurements, but 112 miles sounds more impressive than 180 kilometres) and a 26.2-mile marathon run (if you want that in kilometres, work it out yourself, I can't be bothered). Ironman races take place all over the world and attract hundreds of thousands of people to try and get round the various Iron courses under the cut-off time of 17 hours. People from all walks of life attempt them, from sinewy European professionals who finish in about 8 hours, to massively optimistic overweight Americans who stagger over the line looking like they've been shagged with a ragman's trumpet – and, of course, skinny, obsessive amateurs who spend half the year training for this race at the expense of holidays, puddings, a quiet life, advancement at work, lie-ins, an easy atmosphere at home, any kind of social life, pain-free legs and money.

This particular race is called 'Challenge Roth' – Roth being the name of the nearest town, and 'Challenge' because, for reasons too tedious to go into, it's not allowed to be called an 'official' Ironman, although it takes place over the standard Iron-distance (it's something to with 'Ironman' being a franchise as well as a distance, ya-di-ya-di-yada). Normally when you cross the finish line of an Ironman, some hospital-DJ type with a microphone bellows 'You are an IRONMAN' at you, so I'm wondering what I will have bellowed at me when I finish this race – 'You are a Challenger' makes me sound like an unsuccessful space shuttle, while 'You are a Roth-man' makes me sound like a packet of fags. This is not my first Ironman – in fact it's my tenth since 2006, and I have completed them in such dazzling locations as Florida, Canada, Lake Placid, Nevada, Austria, Lanzarote and, er, Nottingham. So far, I have finished every single one in times ranging from 10 hours 20 minutes (Nottingham) up to 12 hours 45 minutes (Lanza-sodding-rote), although this doesn't make them any less nerve-racking and as we wait for the boom of the starting cannon, my sphincter is going from the size of a five pence piece up to the size of a manhole cover, and back to 5p again.

What makes them so nerve-racking is that they are hard. Perhaps you've done one, in which case you'll appreciate the kind of mystique that I'm trying to build here that we are some kind of race of superheroes whose tri suits should involve a mask, cape, and some sort of badge for our chests. You don't just turn up at the start of these races on the off-chance you'll finish because they will hurt you badly and leave you sagged on the side of the road looking like a deflated testicle. You have to train for months just to make it to the start line in any sort of shape and, once you get there, then there are a million things that can go wrong during the course of 140.6 miles – punctures, dehydration, crashes, panic attacks, injuries, exhaustion, hypothermia, heatstroke, chafed nipples, cramp, the shits, failing to escape the clutches of Scientology and good old fashioned failure

Most of us taking part will be in the 'complete' rather than 'compete' category. The chances are that the race will be won by some professional with a cool name like Faris or Timo or, er, Chrissie, who will finish in 7 hours 59 minutes looking like they've just done a 10k, and who baffle the rest of us by being so good while appearing to have the same number of legs as us. Next will come the ex-pros, sponsored athletes and top end 'age groupers' (as we amateurs are known) who will be seeking the minor prizes like winning their age group – for your further edification the entrants into triathlons are usually divvied up into five-year age groups, so you end up competing against people of similar levels of tooth decay. This crowd will be looking to finish in less than 10 hours, will look a little more dishevelled than the pros but will quickly recover in order to have a good pose around the finishing area in their calf guards, finisher's T-shirt and medal. Looking around me in the water, I can spot a few of these types already and make a mental note to try to thump one or two if the opportunity presents itself – why should I be the only one to feel pain today?

After that will come the phalanx of also-rans whose times range from 10–13 hours and whose bodies range from hefty and muscular to those looking like they need a bloody good dinner, and those of us whose bodies are basically just a collection of fatty deposits and scar tissue. These are the people who have trained hard, executed their race strategy reasonably well, avoided any major catastrophes and for whom the hardest work is yet to come – that of convincing their mates, families and attractive women in pubs that their result was much better than it actually was, using phrases like 'I finished in the top third of the race' or 'I was in the top 50 in my age group.'

Next will come the over-13-hours finishers. Maybe they've had a bad day, maybe it's their first race, maybe they have overcome some huge personal challenge to complete the race, or maybe they're just shit. Either way I always like to give anyone who finishes in this sort of time an extra round of applause (assuming I'm not one of them) because 14 or 15 hours is a bloody long time to be on your feet, let alone swimming, pedalling and staggering about for 140 miles. Another positive side to this group of finishers is that at least they will have the grace to look like they have just done the hardest race on earth and will happily shuffle stiffly over the line caked in snot, dead flies, carelessly applied suncream, a warm paste of energy gels, fruit and perhaps some vomit.

The final group to finish will be those who make it round between 16 and 17 hours. I never know quite how to react to people I see lurching for the line with minutes to spare. Are they celebrating their achievement at becoming an Ironman, or are they crushingly disappointed at their time? Are they smiling, or is that the rictus grin of death brought on by some unspecified pain about their person? Was this what they were expecting, or have they had the worst day since the manager at the Fukushima nuclear plant said 'Sea looks choppy today'? Do they just want to slink away to their bed or are they happy to be damned with faint praise like 'Good effort' or 'Well tried' by smug gits who have already finished? This group tend to look hunted, relieved, slightly rueful and in massive agony in parts of their body I don't want to know about.

All entrants though, no matter how unrealistic their expectations, have one thing in common. Something has drawn us here. Perhaps it's the challenge, perhaps it's the finisher's medal, perhaps it's the fact that you will for evermore be known as an 'Ironman' (though since Robert Downey Jr. got in on the act it's hard to describe yourself as such to kids without coming across as a massive tool), perhaps it's the prize money or perhaps, as in the case of my friend Mark, it's because he hopes it will make girls want to touch his cock.

In my case, it's complicated, which will become apparent throughout this book should you be able to stand to read any further. The title of this book is *Accidental Ironman*, but I don't want to conjure up a picture that I've just wandered up to the start of this race while I was out fetching a paper. The accident in question is more a reference to the fact that I never meant to start doing any of this. For 35 years of my life I had less interest in sports than Louis Spence has in *Nuts* magazine and my presence at these races comes as a constant source of bewilderment to me, and to anyone who has known me longer than the past ten years. Having given it some thought for the purposes of financial gain (this book) I've realised I partly do it for egotistical reasons, partly to make up for previous sporting failures and partly because I thought I'd get the kind of body that meant that my buttocks would be so firm I'd never need to use a nutcracker again. What I've actually ended up with is a body that looks like an anglepoise lamp from Ikea, probably with a name like Tvátt. It is called *Accidental Ironman* because I just sort of drifted into this sport without ever really stopping to wonder what I was doing. Following the fabulous (four times Ironman World Champion) Chrissie Wellington's book *A Life Without Limits* I had contemplated calling it *A Life Without Talents*. Or it could equally have been called *My Struggle*, although I was advised it wouldn't sell so well in Germany. Hopefully, the title does at least go some way to explaining that I don't really know what I'm doing this for and, more specifically, that I don't really know what I'm doing <u>here</u> in the Main Donnau Canal, surreptitiously kicking some French bloke who is trying to nick my start place and generally treating the water around me as my own private country with an incredibly strict immigration policy.

Now you've got this far into the book and I can be

8

absolutely certain you're not some commuter killing time by leafing through the sports books section of the station newsagents (or have I been categorised in comedy – or perhaps 'Bargain Bin'?) we can relax a little and get to know each other some more. Not that this will lead to any lessening of writing standards by the way, oh no, I'm determined you shall have value for your money and if you feel at all short-changed by the quality of words and punctuation I've used please feel free to write to me at: M Brunt, A Yacht, Somewhere, the Bahamas. Anyway, now that we can be free with each other, I am happy to tell you that I'm here because I'm told this particular race is a fast one, and I am thus likely to come away with a very impressive time, always assuming I don't cock it up. I've trained quite hard for this race and my coach Dave, a man about whom you shall hear more, has terrified me with tales of what future training regimes he will put me through should I not return victorious. A couple of years ago the all-conquering Chrissie Wellington set a new record for this course, which made all sorts of people like me put aside our usual below-par work ethic and think 'Hmmmm, I could crack that race out with the usual level of effort and get a much faster time than usual.' Right? We'll see …

I'm also here because I have a bunch of mates who have also been drawn here by the prospect of turning up and knocking out a fast time with the minimum of effort, and the time has come to introduce them to you:

1.  Mark Stewart, a gadget-obsessed sex pest whom I've known for ten years and who has become

one my closest friends, despite him continually, narrowly defeating me in races. Physically he is the tall, sinewy type: if Andy Murray ever went missing for 30 years and the police released one of those e-fits that tried to show him as he'd look at that age, Mark would get rounded up sharpish. He's actually a very good athlete who has the ability to hit his peak fitness for races at exactly the right moment, and a complete inability to complete any race without having to stop at some point to do a massive dump. Mark is starting in one of the waves behind me and is currently flapping about in transition (the area where bikes and kit are stored) trying to sort out a puncture he seems to have acquired on his bike's front tyre (actually the way I've written that 'seems to' implies I am to blame in some kind of Dick Dastardly, race-nobbling act of vandalism, but I swear I was nowhere near his bike your Honour). Mark's least favourite part of the race is the swim and he has been crapping himself all morning about the prospect of being stuck in a canal with a load of neoprene clad knees and elbows, and I have been soothing his nerves by saying things like 'Not much room is there?' and 'Looks punchy to me.'

2.   Joe Reynolds, a man who, on paper, is the most exciting human being in the world given that he is already an Ironman, he works in Formula One racing, and he once appeared in a band on *Top of the Pops* – and a really cool band too; he was

the saxophone player for eighties ska legends The Selecter, playing on their classic anthem 'Three-Minute-Hero', which already gives him masses more credibility than Dustbin Bieber or anyone who's ever slithered into our realm via *The X Factor*. On top of all this, Joe has five daughters – yes, five – all of whom range from loud to absolutely deafening. Joe tends to be at the slower end of the field and is expecting to finish somewhere around the 14–15 hour mark but, to be fair, if you had five gobby daughters you'd want to stay out on the course and get a bit of peace and quiet, too. Physically Joe is the short, sinewy type and in terms of what he looks like, picture if you can a slightly bewildered looking Ferrero Rocher. Joe is currently swimming for his life because he is in one of the waves in front of me, and he too likes the swim part of the race least of all. I have been soothing his nerves all morning by saying things like 'I wonder how long it will take me to catch you and swim over the top of you?'

3. Steve McMenamin, a gristle-kneed former-rugby-player-turned-swimmer who hails from that well known part of Ireland known as Coventry. Steve is someone I seem to have known all my life, although I can't actually remember when I met him. As well as being one of the funniest people on the planet he constantly baffles me with how he managed to persuade his wife, Kay, to marry him, given how nice she is. Steve now lives in Brighton

and once persuaded me to swim the Channel with him (more on that later). He's also the only Olympic Torchbearer I know, having carried it through Sussex for a mile, trying desperately to ignore the mobile phone constantly going off in his pocket with texts from me, Mark and his other mates urging him to be the first person to trip over, drop it or set fire to the next runner. Steve is an extremely good swimmer and is also out there somewhere ahead of me, ploughing through the field and any unfortunate flounderers in his way, and is probably relieved to be under way to escape the jokes about being India's number-one triathlete. Before leaving home he ordered some Irish flags for his family to wave, only to open them in Germany and discover that he'd been sent Indian flags by mistake, so as far as we were concerned he is the subcontinent's sole representative in the race and he has endured four solid days of curry-based piss-taking.

And then there's me, Martyn Brunt, currently awaiting the cannon's boom while burdened with the weight of expectation and teetering on the edge of self-befoulment. Through years of self-sacrifice and gritty determination I have carved out a reputation as one of the sport's top mediocre performers, whose only talent appears to be being able to tolerate limitless amounts of pain (although not my own). My kicking has seen off Monsieur Froggy and as the seconds tick down to the start it occurs to me to wonder whatever happened to Katie Laws who was the first girl I fancied at school, what the capital of Peru is, and is it just me who thinks that Alan Sugar looks like a dog's bollock balanced on top of a suit? None of this has any relevance to the race I'm about to do, but it just goes to show how your mind wanders when you're nervous.

I check my watch, wondering whether to start it now or leave it until the cannon actually goes off so I will know to the precise second how much I'm failing my target times by throughout the race. These final seconds before the start are the closest you will feel to your fellow competitors, a kinship based on shared suffering, shared nerves, shared effort and the shared joy that completing this kind of event weirdly brings you. Triathlon is an egalitarian sport that makes little distinction between the poor (me), the rich (my friend Neill Morgan), the exciting (Jenson Button), the dull (Neill again), the upper classes (my friend Will Kirk-Wilson), the lower classes (anyone from Bedworth), the good (Chrissie Wellington), the bad (Ponce Armstrong), the old (Alistair Brownlee), the young (Jonny Brownlee), the fat (my friend Tony Nutt), the thin (Tony's hair), the popular (Spencer Smith) and the friendless (me after this). I like to think that something we've got in common is a vague sense of wonderment about why we're doing this. Why get up at 5.00 a.m. to go swimming? Why give up a nice cozy bed to go cycling for hours in all weathers? Why go swimming in a freezing lake? Why run so far or fast that you virtually collapse? Why give up your night out because you are too tired to move – or because you have to train the next morning?

Like most triathletes in training for an Ironman, I never really dwell on 'why', being naturally more interested in 'what'. What was my time for that last lap? What is the weather going to be like for the ride? What kit should I wear? What can I do to get stronger towards the end of races? What will happen to my weight if I eat that biscuit? What is the price of those wheels? The only 'why' that I've ever dwelt on is 'why don't girls seem impressed when I tell them about my marathon splits at the end of an Ironman … ?' However, at the start of any race there's nothing like having the feeling you've bitten off more than you can chew to give you a moment of self-awareness and to question what on earth you think you are doing! Am I here because I want to fit in? There's certainly part of me that enjoys fitting in with people whose athletic achievements I admire, and I enjoy listening to someone talking about being 'on the rivet on the K10/10 in a 53/12' and knowing exactly what they are talking about. Or am I here because I want to stand apart? Try as I might I can't help but glow with smugness when I hear someone talk about going to the gym or jogging a Park Run as the pinnacle of their fitness without thinking 'Christ, that's not even a warm-up!' And, yes, I confess to feeling shameless superiority when I'm out in public and I see the undulating blob monsters waddling their way into certain tax-averse coffee shops and fast food chain restaurants, taking pleasure in thinking 'I'm not like you – and plug up your tophole fatty, you're eating too much.'

Frankly, I don't know, but I wish I could understand, why I've been so cold while cycling that frost formed on me, so hot after running that I jumped into someone's ornamental fish pond, and so tired I've fallen asleep in a plate of food. I've been soaked and sunburned; I've had heatstroke and hypothermia; I've crashed, fallen, punctured, tripped, collapsed, been hopelessly lost, had endless bollockings from my wife for being late for things, been lectured by a beach lifeguard for 'causing distress to the public' and cautioned by the police for exposing myself to a passing coachload of pensioners while urinating up a tree. Maybe by the end of this book my reasons for participating in this nonsense will be clearer to both of us (not that you give a toss probably but I'd like to know).

And is it just me that wonders why, in the name of sweet baby Jesus, I'm about to do what I'm about to do? As the last few seconds of inactivity tick by, I can't help but wonder how big Katie Law's breasts are these days and whether anyone else out there is an *Accidental Ironman*.

BOOM!

# Chapter 2

Steve Elliot
Craig Freer
Mark Edwards
Graham Harris

Okay, there go the good footballers. I expected them to be picked first because, even at the age of seven, they have that easy ability to control a ball with their feet without looking at them, a handy turn of pace, the ability to make space for themselves and the confident swagger that comes with being good at something that everyone wants to be good at. The bastards. Steve especially has talent and will go on to play at county level and be scouted by Coventry City before vanishing somewhere into the masses of kids who don't make it, possibly as a result of pissing his talent up the wall. He's good, knows it, and behaves accordingly, treating weedier kids with disdain and having girls waiting to carry his bag for him. Craig too has talent and will also go on to play at secondary school and county level. He's less showy than Steve but a more prolific goal-scorer and much nicer with it, which makes his loss to cancer as a teenager all the sadder. Every kid has their nemesis at junior school, and Mark Edwards was mine for a time. The same age as me, similar looks to me, same interests as me, lived very close to me and our parents knew each other, which meant we often went on day trips together. We were sort-of friends in an uneasy kind of way, but rivals too and the occasional fights between us tended to be more vicious than any fights with other kids. And of course he was a much, much better footballer than me.

Darren Rose
Guy Slater

And there go the goalkeepers. Again, no surprise that they have been selected by the respective team captains picking their teams from the knot of pale, scrawny schoolboys standing on a muddy football pitch behind the main school building. Teams need goalkeepers and these two seem keen to do it, although Darren is actually quite good. I am not good as a goalkeeper, being poor at catching, kicking and throwing and disliking being in the way of a wet leather ball that assumes the weight and velocity of a small planet when slogged at you from ten yards away. Guy was my best friend at junior school, which meant we spent a lot of time riding bikes together and fighting. A local farmer's son, I can still picture him wearing the same baggy, grey home-knitted sweater to school every day (this was the early seventies when home-made clothes were standard stuff). Why he wanted to be a goalie I can't imagine and we lost touch soon after we went to different secondary schools, though his absence from any First Division teams throughout the eighties and nineties suggests he may have dropped his interest soon after – as well as seemingly dropping every cross I recall him flailing for.

Timothy Lloyd
David Homer
John Kerr
Craig Burden

Fair enough, these are the fast running kids who seem happy enough to peg it up and down the pitch all afternoon. Timothy is the short, squat, burly type of sprinter; David the tall, long striding choppy-handed sort; John his short-arsed equivalent and Craig the bandy-legged sort who looks like an egg-whisk when he runs. Every team needs players with pace, although ball control is definitely a secondary consideration to speed with these four. Tim is a nice lad whose mum knows my mum and who regularly plays at my house, David too is an inoffensive, slight sort of kid who seems more keen on being a runner than playing football. John is a spiteful little turd who should change his first name to 'Juan', while Craig is the other candidate I have for 'best friend at school' and is one of those cheery rascal types who always seems to be up to something but gets away with it by being cheeky and funny. He also has an older brother who is his chief supplier of *Penthouse* and *Knave* magazines.

Robert Greenway
Christian French
Richard Lee
Paul Randle

Hmm. These are more your solid, workmanlike types, not particularly skilful but able to control a ball, pass it, and head it without squinting or shrinking their heads into their necks like a turtle. I'm not particularly surprised these have been picked ahead of me because they definitely try harder than I do and get more involved in any game of football than I do. In my mind's eye both Robert and Christian have massive heads (physically I mean, I'm not suggesting they bragged a lot), which may account for their abilities in the air. I don't remember much about Richard and Paul other than a vague memory of them believing that they were much better at football than they actually were. Paul went to the same secondary school as me but we were in different classes so we might as well have been different Zimbabwean political parties for all the contact we had with each other.

Michael Morton
Paul Morton
Kevin Harborne
Harman Howland
Shaun Lester

Okay, I had maybe half-hoped I might have been picked ahead of a couple of these because I am slightly self-delusional and because we're now getting down among the crappier choices. None of these five has any particular footballing ability although, to be fair, they are at least keen on the sport. Kevin particularly wants nothing more than to be a professional footballer and lives near Coventry City winger Tommy Hutchison, making him a popular supplier of autographs, written in suspiciously childlike handwriting. Sadly, he is denied his dream by being as good at football as Girls Aloud are at pot-holing. Michael and Paul are the most competitive pair of siblings since Venus and Serena Williams, and it's a toss-up whether it's safest to have them on opposite sides kicking lumps out of each other, or on the same side kicking lumps out of others. And each other.

Mitchell Edwards
Robert Fox
Darren Miles
Shaun Moorcroft

Now I'm worried and any ego I had developed by the age of seven has been seriously bruised that I have not been picked in with this group. Mitchell Edwards can run fast but isn't interested, Robert is ponderous and couldn't hit a cow's arse with a banjo, and Shaun's only claim to fame is to be a cousin of Great Britain's star Olympic runner and Coventry Godiva Harrier Dave Moorcroft. (As an aside, I now know Dave well, having become a Godiva Harrier myself, and he tells me there is no Shaun Moorcroft in his family, the little liar). Every street has its trouble family, and the Mileses are the trouble family in ours. Of the four sons, Darren is the worst so I can only assume he has been picked ahead of me through fear, although his team will soon be a man down after he gets sent off for hacking someone down, calling the teacher a wanker, or just jumping over the fence and running off.

And so, we are down to the last two, and their names are Andrew Owen and Martyn Brunt. The former is a timid but funny kid whose Italian mum used to stand at the school gates at home-time shouting: 'Annderrrew, Annderrrew, hurrrry up or you getta no sweets' and who had, according to Andrew, a 'wooden buster'. And then we have Martyn, the worst footballer you will ever see in your life. Not only does he not particularly like the game, but he lacks even the most basic of skills, seemingly unable to control his feet without having to stare at them, unable to summon up the energy to leave the ground when jumping, and believing that the best tactic is simply to follow the ball around the pitch – or more accurately follow where the ball has just been around the pitch. Andrew and Martyn are the last two kids standing on the muddy pitch behind the main school building. The team captains would be quite happy not to select either of them but are forced to by the PE teacher, so it's now an exercise in damage limitation. Which of these two will be the least inept? The captains are receiving words of advice from their assembled team about the various pitfalls of picking either one of them, and in truth whoever is picked will have as much impact on any game as Darren Anderton had on, er, any game. However, it does matter. It matters very much to Andrew and Martyn because neither one of them wants to be 'Last Pick' – the lowest of the low, rejected by all. Whoever is picked will sprint over to their new team, pathetically grateful for the crumb of consolation they have been fed. Whoever is not picked will not even have their name called out, they will just be stared at accusingly by the captain lumbered with them who will just say, 'Come on then' before turning and running off. And then it comes …

Andrew

If you grew up in the early seventies as I did, then this particular form of torture may be familiar to you. PE lessons consisted solely of football played between teams of about 25-a-side with a ball so heavy that if punted at you it would probably take your head clean off your shoulders. Teams were picked by choosing two captains (normally the two best players) and lining them up facing the clutch of skinny, malnourished bags of bones they had to choose from, whereupon the captains would make their selections by pointing at their chosen players with increasing indifference as they went through the ranks. Inevitably the best players got hoovered up first, and then so on until it was just me and some kid with a built-up shoe. This sadism was presided over by the PE teacher, Mr Williams – football fanatic and all-round bastard, and possessor of a tiny head yet enormous nose with cavernous nostrils.

Mr Williams was Welsh and, this being the early seventies meant that Welsh rugby was in its pomp. Mr Williams, though, was from north Wales and a 'devotee of the round ball', which meant we got nothing but football all year round. This was pretty good news for most kids because it was the era of the first superstar footballers of Manchester United, Liverpool and Arsenal, with players like Kevin Keegan, Lou Macari, the Greenhoffs, Steve Heighway, David Fairclough, Sammy McIlroy, Charlie George, Malcolm Macdonald et al, struggling to get off the ground under the weight of their sideburns and growing perms so big that they obscured entire stands. Even Coventry City – my team – had a couple of good players, with Ian Wallace and his huge, ginger, bepermed scalp dazzling defenders, along with the aforementioned Tommy Hutchison, who could probably still get in the side now if he fancied it.

This football focus also had its drawbacks. My school, Allesley County Primary, lay in a village right on the outskirts of Coventry and each year it would hold a school sports day full of such athletic events such as the 100m sprint, long jump into a dogshit-filled sandpit, shot-put with a beanbag, high jump over a couple of poles and a rope, and a longer run of some unspecified distance that involved a lap of the playing field. No training was done for this because Mr Williams didn't like anything that wasn't football, so our school was not generally a hotbed of athletic achievement. In fact, about the only non-football exercise we got as kids in the early seventies was from trying to outrun creepy TV celebrities. We did get to have a go at the occasional alternative sport and I vividly remember that in the wake of Virginia Wade's win at Wimbledon we had a 'tennis lesson' – which involved trying to hit an airstream ball against a wall with a wooden paddle. If you managed it twice you could have lessons, and if you didn't it was back to the classroom and don't let the doorknob hit you in the arse on the way out. Needless to say I was back inside doing times tables before you could say 'Navratilova' and a possible future tennis great was lost to the sport, athough sitting on 'Brunty's Bulge' doesn't sound quite as appealing as 'Henman Hill'.

What I've done in the past couple of pages is to try to set the scene for the rest of this book (and, perhaps, pique the interest of any passing psychiatrist) by underlining that, from a very early age, I was deemed as being *shit at sports*. Mostly this was because I was *shit at sports*, although I grew up slightly resentful of the fact that I was deemed *shit at sports* because I was shit at football. It was some years before people learned that I was also shit at rugby, cricket, hockey, athletics, squash and tennis. Whether I was shit at them because I already lacked self-belief in my sporting abilities, or because I was genuinely shit at them, is one of those chicken-and-egg debates. Actually, no it isn't. We're friends now and I can truthfully confess to you that I was indeed *shit at sports*.

Things did not improve when I went to secondary school – although at least I was spared the hated football, because at my new grammar school they didn't play it, no doubt considering it a pastime for pikeys and chavs. Instead – horror of horrors – they played rugby. I didn't think it was possible for me to dislike playing any sport more than football, but I quickly realised how wrong I was the first time we were made to play rugby. It took precisely one lesson for the sports master to work out exactly who were going to be the gentlemen in the team in the years to come and who was going to be condemned to fruitlessly farting around on the outfield with the 'other ranks' for the next fifteen school terms. The rugby team at school seemed to be populated entirely by thick-necked, slow-witted types called Ollie or Will, and their attitude towards those of us who weren't interested in rugby – as well as their general attitude towards girls, art, music, any sport that wasn't rugby, anyone slightly camp and thus a bit gay, and anyone with vaguely dark skin – did not make me yearn for their company.

On the plus side, though, the sports master, Mr Jones (another Welshman, although at least this one was the real deal, having played rugby for Wales), didn't want us lightweights getting in the way of his fit, committed, well-drilled bunch of homophobic racists. So we were spared the humiliation of having to play in the same games as them, and were instead banished to the fringes of the playing fields where we were made to play endless games of rugby, largely at walking pace and supervised by the music teacher, Mr Sutton. He was probably as uninterested in the whole process as we were – and at least we got to stand around with our hands on our knackers when it got cold, which he couldn't do without ending up on some kind of register.

In the summer term, thank the Lord, the school switched to cricket – which was at least a sport I liked, albeit still one I was shit at. This was a new experience for me and I recall my first feelings of frustration that here was something I liked, wanted to do, and yet couldn't get into the school team because of a crippling lack of talent. I was bloody awful at batting – the highlight of my batting career being a match-winning stand of 51 with a lad called Jamie Walker, with him getting 50. However, I was a reasonable fielder and, dare I say it, a not entirely bad bowler, capable of maiden overs and the odd wicket. I didn't have a particular style, although I had one delivery that was a full toss that used to lure batsmen into taking a big swing, only for the ball to suddenly drop from its trajectory like a turd dropping out the back of a cow and flop past their swishing bat on to the wicket. Around the time that I was at my most keen there was a programme on the television called *Bodyline*, which dramatised the controversial England victory in the Ashes in Australia when Douglas Jardine's men started pelting Don Bradman and the Aussies in the ribs and faces. The bowling attack was led by fast bowlers Harold Larwood and Bill Voce, and I became obsessed with turning myself into the next Larwood. I spent hours in the back garden slinging balls at the shed, giving myself a back so hunched my mum started ironing my shirts with a wok and I had to stick my thumb up my arse to get my school tie on. This attempt at becoming the next Fred Trueman petered out eventually, leading to precisely no wickets but ending with the satisfying achievement of hitting my friend Paul Etherington squarely in the balls with a full toss that saw him plummet to the ground and vomit lavishly all over the stumps.

I should point out at this moment that I am not a descendant of a particularly sporty line. My mum was a figure-skater and gymnast when young, making her by far the most accomplished sportsperson in the whole family, and she actually met my dad while ice skating when he swept her off her feet. I don't mean this romantically, I mean he literally swept her off her feet by crashing into her.

My dad's sporting talents were less obvious. Throughout my childhood he claimed to be a tennis player of some renown and we used to play games together in my early teens. However, after he passed away a few years ago my mum debunked the myth that he was any good by saying that he was deemed the best player of their circle of friends simply because he possessed a racket with all the strings in it, had tennis balls that hadn't had all the hair thwacked off them, and didn't have a fag on the go while playing, unlike my Uncle Toms (plural). Throughout his whole life I never knew him to break into a run, and I only ever saw him swim once when we went on holiday to America and he swam by bobbing about face down in a San Diego swimming pool like the body from an improperly weighted Mafia hit. He did own a bike, but his idea of cycling was to pedal uphill to the next village three miles away with Uncle Tom number one, stop at the Bull and Butcher pub, and then freewheel all the way home. On the occasions that I was allowed to go along on my Raleigh Commando bike (with twist-grip gears in the handlebars no less) I was usually away off at the front on the way up the hill, made to sit outside with a lemonade during pub time, and then left for dead on the way back as they hurtled back down the hill, Uncle Tom only stopping if his Benson and Hedges went out.

Even my wider family lacked any sporting heroes. My Grandad Jack was a physical training instructor in the army until a German machine-gunner put paid to his kneecaps, although this didn't stop him cycling between Birmingham and Walsall every morning after the war to his job as a steam engine driver. As he said himself, all that metal around his legs made him much better at playing the spoons. Grandad Albert had played some football in his time but his real passion was gardening. He grew the largest vegetables that the Birmingham Council allotments ever saw. I would spend hours with him in his garden, watching him swapping trays of seedlings with fellow green-fingered enthusiasts to the extent that I grew up thinking that seeds and cuttings were some

27

sort of illicit currency. Later in life he was frustrated by his inability to do the things he used to do – like bomb the Japanese.

The only other member of my family worth mentioning is my cousin Sharon, who was so fat that if she fell on her back she'd rock herself to sleep trying to get back up again. At one point she topped 20 stone and this was back in the seventies when seeing fat biffers waddling around with their bum cracks on show was unusual enough to be worthy of comment from passers-by. We were not close as cousins due to her being a good bit older than me, and a spoilt miserable sow – you'd think if someone is going to be overweight then at least they'd have the common decency to be jolly. I well remember coming home one day from school to be met by my dad standing in the drive, looking very solemn and saying: 'You know how your cousin Sharon was told to lose five stone or die? Well I'm very sorry to tell you that … she's lost five stone.'

My dad was a man of many talents, mostly associated with fine wine, jazz, elegant suits and being extremely popular. There was one sport he was committed to though, and that was golf. American comedian Robin Williams once described golf as the only time a white man can dress like a black pimp and get away with it, and my dad took this to extremes, cutting a singular figure at Coventry's Hearsall Golf Club in his red plus-fours, argyle socks, diamond-patterned Pringle sweater and large American baseball cap. Like most club golfers he was mildly obsessed with the game and all the cupboards in our house seemed to be full of individually wrapped Slazenger golf balls. I wish I'd kept a few now because they're dead handy for rolling around under your foot if you've got plantar fascitis.

In truth, he wasn't a bad player and reached a handicap of about 10. Once he even won a club trophy, in which Mum used to keep her sewing kit, much to his annoyance. Inevitably I was also drawn into this world and was given my first set of clubs at the age of about six, and given 'lessons' by my dad. Dad was not the most patient of souls, and 'lessons' would mostly involve watching me hack away at the ball like a lumberjack attacking a tree whereupon he would bellow 'NOOOO! Like this!!!', grab the club off me and then proceed to shank the ball into some trees before claiming I had 'put him off.'

In recalling this, I've just remembered the one and only time Dad tried to teach me to play cricket when I was about eight. God knows why he did this because he couldn't play the game for toffee but he decided that he would bowl and I would bat, whereupon he launched a ball at me that Jimmy Anderson would be proud of and which cracked me so hard on the shin that it made me dry heave. Unfortunately for him, my mum had just wandered into the garden and witnessed the spectacle of her son being poleaxed, whereupon she raced across the lawn with a roar, tore one of the stumps out of the ground and flung it at my dad like a Zulu warrior, spearing him in the knee. He collapsed howling in agony and was locked out of the house while I was carried inside for ice cream and sympathy.

Actually, I wasn't bad at golf and managed to battle my way to a single-figure handicap, although I was never a natural and didn't enjoy it enough to do any practising. I was capable of the odd good round and was particularly good at driving off the tee and belting the ball for miles down the fairway. The trouble was I used to putt the same way. I ended up playing most weeks with Dad from the age of about eight all the way through to my mid-thirties when he became too ill to stay out on the course for long. I still miss those rounds with him, crushed as I was by the embarrassment of walking down a fairway next to a man in multicoloured knickerbockers and a flat cap with a bobble on it. I never won anything, and in fact the only real highlight I remember was once playing with a pro called Tim Rouse and some other friends at a course called Hollinwell in Nottinghamshire. Hollinwell was very nice and very posh, with a final hole that finished right in front of a large clubhouse with a huge conservatory and patio. I had had an atrocious round, spraying balls all over the shop and playing what was generally known as 'Military Golf' (left, right, left, right). Having done nothing of any note for the whole game, on the final hole I produced a shot of dazzling brilliance that pitched in the centre of the green with backspin and rolled up to about two inches from the pin. As we walked on to the green the patio was thronged with people having their evening gin and tonics, and I received a round of applause from the crowd, politely acknowledging it with a modest wave when I walked over to my ball. This led Tim to turn to me and say: 'you wanker.'

University is often the place where people discover or build on their sporting passions, but I continued my indifference all the way through my studies. I spent three years at Liverpool University between 1986 and

1989, having scraped there courtesy of an A-level in General Studies, which is the equivalent of being given a certificate after a pub quiz. I elected to prolong my education and be surrounded by girls and subsidised entertainment, rather than go straight to work in an office, factory or meat storage facility. During this period the only time I remember ever getting sweaty was while trying to unhook a girl's bra, so it seems inexplicable that on returning to Coventry (Christ knows why) after my degree I decided to have another go at ... football. Quite how I thought this would end I have no idea, and if I was hoping that the twelve-year gap between leaving junior school and starting work had suddenly imbued me with some kind of footballing ability, then I was in for a rude awakening.

What happened was that I was approached by a bloke in a pub I used to drink in called the Windmill and asked if I wanted to turn out for the pub side. His name was Steve Brassington and he was trying to put a team together, having decamped there from another nearby pub called the Sportsman's Arms (pound a pint and a stripper on a Sunday). Having been given £100 by the landlord to buy some new kit with the pub's name on it, we promptly pissed this windfall up the wall on a night out and then turned out for our first game of the season in the old Sportsman's kit with the name taped over. At our first training session, Brasso quickly realised the awful mistake he'd made in asking me to join the team, and I was moved from striker, to midfield general, to centre half, to right back, to substitute in the space of about five minutes flat. Pace, flair, skill and vision were just some of the traits completely absent from the team, but even in this company I stood out as a fat, lumbering oaf of no discernible use unless there was a chronic shortage of people with a pulse to turn out. Despite all this I quite enjoyed being part of the team while it lasted, chiefly because of some of the characters it featured, including:

Tom Sefton – an alcoholic goalkeeper who used to turn up Sunday mornings shaking with the DTs and who'd say things like 'Don't let 'em get any crosses in lads, I've got a bastard of a headache.'

Will Johnson – a ponderous striker known as 'Shovel Foot' for being the scourge of side-netting, or 'Jigsaw' because he frequently went to pieces in the box.

Simon Dale – known as 'Black Bess' because he galloped fruitlessly up and down the wing in search of the ball, or 'Gunshot' because of his habit of shooting at goal whenever he got the ball, no matter where he was on the pitch.

Chris Morris – Moggy was actually a good player and a lovely guy unless riled, at which point he'd turn into a combination of Vinnie Jones and Reinhard Heydrich until he'd upended someone, whereupon he'd return to being Penry the mild-mannered janitor.

Steve Ward – Wardrobe was a somewhat static defender, also known as 'Douglas Bader' for being good in the air but crap on the ground.

Greg Evans – a classy midfielder who later ended up in the clink for donning a raincoat, cap and glasses and collecting his dad's pension for two years after he died.

We played in the heady heights of the Bedworth and North Coventry Sunday Alliance Division One and in 1992 actually managed to go through a whole season unbeaten. I made a number of substitute appearances (the number in question being four) totalling about 25 minutes of actual play in which I managed to touch the ball a couple of times but, more importantly, I managed not to cock anything up either, which was my main goal. Sadly, after securing promotion to the Premier Division, the team fizzled out and was reincarnated as a five-a-side outfit, a game even more fast-paced and bad-tempered than ordinary football, in which my need to still keep looking at my feet to control them was horribly exposed on the one occasion I tried it.

And that's about it by way of sporting background and context-setting, so if you've picked up this book in search of the inspirational story of someone who overcame the odds to succeed, then you're in for a disappointing read (and you may be in for one even if you aren't looking for that). I have neither overcome odds, nor particularly succeeded. I have not challenged a disability, beaten the bullies, battled through setbacks, defeated schizophrenia by defying the voices in my head (either of them), or picked up the pieces of my shattered dreams and rebuilt them into a towering monolith of success. People do not throw rose petals at me as I walk down the street nor do I drink champagne from a golden slipper, which is probably just as well as I don't want to die of greenfly or damp feet. I was just a nice, inoffensive kid who happened to be shit at sports. Except one ...

# Chapter 3

It is 4.45 a.m. and the bedside alarm has just gone off, producing much the same effect as if I had been blasted in the coccyx with a taser. I spend the next five minutes lying in bed in a state of advanced death until the alarm goes off again, prompting me to sit up slowly, like a zombie rising from the grave, only even more furious and incoherent.

What follows looks like a mime artist attempting to portray the world's most incompetent burglar as I stumble around the bedroom in the dark trying to put on socks, pants and shirt, all while also trying to stay completely silent for fear of waking my wife, Nicky. She will not be pleased if she is disturbed and can be reeeally grumpy if she doesn't get enough sleep. I once did a radio interview in which the DJ asked how I managed to get up so early in the morning to go training, to which I joked, 'If you'd seen my wife first thing in the morning you'd want to get out of bed as well,' which got a laugh but boy did I get in trouble for that one.

I sneak downstairs like a dog up to no good and slink past my dog, Patch, who really has been up to no good and who is now watching me beadily through one open eye as I try to make myself a drink and a bowl of cereal. Normally I am pretty bad at staying silent in the kitchen and this morning is no exception, although not as bad as a few nights ago when I returned home 'refreshed' from the pub and set about making myself an amazingly large fry-up at 2.00 a.m. using every single pan in the kitchen. Then I pad quietly outside to my campervan, trying not to wake the neighbours, and start the engine. Actually, bollocks to the neighbours … they never care whether I'm asleep or not, so I rev the engine and screech off up the road, as impressively as one can in a Mazda Bongo.

The reason for all this creeping around is that I am off swimming with my local swimming club – or Masters Swimming Club to be precise as the adults team is known, to differentiate us from the juniors and seniors. They have separate training times away from the grown-ups lest they should have to share a changing room with us and end up running screaming from the pool at the sight of several saggy scrotums resembling the last turkeys in the butcher's shop window.

The swims take place in Coventry's main sports centre, or 'Coventry Baths' as it is better known, which happens to be one of the few 50-metre pools in Britain despite the Council's persistent attempts to turn it into some kind of tiresome splash pool. There are seven swimming sessions on offer to members of the City of Coventry Swimming Club each week, two of which take place from 5.30– 7.00 a.m., which is why I'm up with the lark and wrestling the turkey into my budgie-smugglers. The reason for starting so early is because the pool is not open to the great unwashed public until 7.00 a.m., so this way we get to have some quality training time without having to dodge round some old gimmer who blocks the lane by hanging in the water like a bloody jellyfish. The session is presided over by Allison Stoney, former international swimmer, multiple medal winner and highly respected ASA coach, who possesses the most important qualification any swim coach can have – that of having a voice like an estuary foghorn that can be heard even when your head is under water. This morning's session involved a warm-up of 8 x 150m freestyle (yes, that's a *warm-up* of 1200m!), followed by a prep set of 1,000m worth of drills, before the main set of 2,000m worth of 100m and 50m sprints punctuated by recovery swims of backstroke and fly. By the time we are done I feel as though someone has spent the past ninety minutes hitting my upper arms with a frying pan, and I have clenched my jaw so hard to achieve Allison's target times that the enamel may have dropped off my teeth. Allison is a hardened swim coach of the old school who operates a competitive Masters team, but she doesn't mind a few triathletes joining in with the sessions provided we also turn out for the club in relay teams in big national galas. Sharing the lane with me this morning is fellow triathlete Keith Burdett, a silver-haired freestyle powerhouse who looks like a bleached Wookie. This session is not unusually hard by Allison's standards. No matter what she throws at us we keep turning up like we've all got Stockholm Syndrome.

I mentioned that I was shit at all sports except one, and that one is swimming. I was actually a reasonably good swimmer as a kid and swam for City of Coventry as a junior and teenager until girls, going out, girls, drinking and girls began to occupy my time. As ever with me, it wasn't a straightforward story; as a toddler I apparently hated the water, screaming the pool down as my dad towed me round in a rubber ring making chugging noises

– although this may of course have been because he was wearing some multicoloured knickerbocker trunks. At the age of seven, though, I broke my leg after dicking about on a hillside with some other kids and once I'd left hospital after eight weeks in traction, the doctors told my parents that swimming was the best way to get me up to strength, so I was packed off to Livingstone Road Baths to kick my way up and down the pool. This time I took to swimming like a duck to hoisin sauce and soon I was in the team in galas, enduring that horrible moment of total silence you get just before a race starts while you're standing on the blocks bricking yourself.

Now forgive me if I digress for a moment but this is MY book. Okay, you've paid for it so technically it's yours, but this is my only chance to get something off my chest that has been on there for almost 40 years. My leg-breaking incident took place at my junior school during playtime and was caused by me falling awkwardly after being pushed down a hill. The fall not only broke my leg but also knocked me unconscious and when I came to I was being dragged – yes, *dragged* – by the shoulders by two older kids into the assembly hall under the supervision of one of the teachers. Once in there I was laid flat on my back on one of those long wooden benches whereupon the teacher, now accompanied by another teacher and presumably fellow member of the Hitler Youth, tried to *straighten my leg out*. Needless to say I screamed the place down, leading them to declare my leg was broken. I was then carried to the entrance hall, sat in a chair with my bent leg propped on a table, while they phoned not an ambulance, but my mum to come and pick me up.

Mum was left to carry me to her car alone, lie me on the back seat and drive me to Coventry and Warwickshire Hospital where a passing stranger helped her carry me into A&E where I spent the next eight weeks. I don't remember seeing either of these teachers again after this, presumably because my dad went up to the school and killed them with one of his golf clubs.

Anyway, violent recriminations aside, I carried on swimming with a modicum of success until my mid-teens, but drifted away from the sport until my mid-thirties when taking up triathlons made me start the old early-morning torture again. Unusually for a triathlete, swimming is my favourite part of the race. All the coolest animals in the world swim. Sharks swim, as do dolphins, whales, otters, seals, penguins, clownfish, manta-rays, seahorses, manatees, duck-billed platypuses, Sharron Davies, dreadful spindly killer-fish and, of course, Ironmen in training. Let's be honest, swimming is what makes triathletes special, because it scares the crap out of ordinary people. If I had a pound for every non-triathlete who told me they could 'do the bike and run but couldn't manage 40m never mind 400', well I'd have about a tenner, but you get the picture. For most people a few lengths of semi-drowning in their local pool is enough without adding the concepts of open water, wetsuits and getting booted in the face. Consequently, if you want to stand tall among mere mortals as a fearless giant with a granite jaw that could deflect kettles being hurled at your head, it's the swim that will do it for you.

Even among experienced triathletes, the swim is often something to be endured rather than enjoyed and for newbies it's the part of triathlon that has them sweating more than Peter Andre on *University Challenge*. Neither Mark nor Joe, my fellow Challenge Roth-men, are relishing the swim while for me it's going to be easily the best bit of the whole race. Having spent a lot of time paddling about, I have acquired the following tips about triathlon-swimming, which I now pass on to you at no extra charge.

Tip 1 – Choose your swim cap carefully
Just as triathletes spend ages selecting the right race T-shirt to wear to intimidate others with evidence of their athletic brilliance, the same goes for swim hats. A cap with a race name on it trumps a plain one, and any cap with Ironman on it trumps that. The only thing that trumps an Ironman cap is a swimming club hat, because it marks you out as someone who enjoys this kind of thing. The only exception to all this is bald men who can swim bareheaded. It's one of the few occasions where being a baldy is an advantage – no cap to worry about, no towel, no shampoo, just a quick half-hour cry in front of the mirror and you're ready.

Tip 2 – Join a club
Rebecca Adlington did not become a champion by having to battle past a fat bloke doing widths, and neither will you. With lakes and seaside out of bounds for six months of the year, a swimming pool is the best place to get the metres in, which inevitably means mixing it with the public doing breaststroke in the fast lane. Take it from me, no matter how

many times you splash or 'accidentally' kick them, they never get the message. So you're much better off joining your local club where you can acquire that lovely permanent chlorine smell after hours of untroubled pull-buoy reps.

Tip 3 – Learn to fly or tumble
If you must share your training time with the public, creating a bit of room for yourself is vital. Nothing says 'Piss off out of my way' more than doing butterfly or tumble turns. Neither will help you in a triathlon, but they are an important skill for keeping the head-out-of-the-water-don't-get-my-hair-wet brigade at bay.

Tip 4 – Avoid cold-water weirdos
When you start training in lakes and seas, you will notice some people stand out from the rubber-clad crowd by wearing nothing but a costume that gives all the cold-protection of a Borat-style mankini. These are open-water swimmers who are training for some ridiculous venture like swimming to Denmark, and no matter how freezing the water, these people always claim to feel warm, in the way that people are when they carry a bit too much weight. Have nothing to do with these dangerous lunatics, because I know to my cost they will talk you into some kind of salty torture. This has happened to me, as we shall see in a moment when I was talked into joining a Channel swim, and which was the worst idea I've had since I tried to convince some girls that I could speak Japanese by shoving some really hot chips in my mouth.

Tip 5 – Make your decision about the Piranha Pack
The piranha pack is that collection of triathletes who start on the front row of the race, charge into the water at full tilt and spend the next 750m/1500m/3.8k cheerfully beating each other up. These are not places for the faint-hearted and even as an experienced swimmer I once got duffed up so much that when I went for a medical examination the doctor started doing a post-mortem. However, the pack always takes the shortest line so you have to decide whether to join the punchy fun for the quickest route, or stay well out of it and take a longer way round.

These tips won't give you superhero powers, but they may help you survive in the water a little bit more easily, and we don't need any superheroes anyway, there are already enough people out on the streets of Britain fighting each other in their pants. There's no doubt that all my pool training has helped my triathlon swimming enormously although, on the downside, it has led me to start taking part in a number of Masters swimming galas. For the unknowing among you, Masters swimming tournaments are open to 24-year-olds and over – and in many cases quite a long way over. In fact, some of the competitors don't look like they're pushing forty, they look like they're dragging it. They are run along exactly the same lines as all those swimming tournaments you see on the telly, although sadly without the opportunity to talk to Sharron Davies at the end while wearing nothing but a pair of Speedos. Distances vary from 50m sprints up to 1500m death-battles, and you can choose between the different strokes of front crawl, breast-struggle, back-struggle and butter-flop. A typical advert for a Masters swim gala could easily read: 'Hey you! Are you old enough to pay income tax and go to bed at a time of your own choosing? When you swim, can you dive in without knocking yourself unconscious and do a tumble-turn without half the pool going up your nose? Do you fancy the idea of walking around with more gold round your neck than Mr T? Then it's Masters swimming for you!'

Because I'm over 40 and farcically competitive, Allison talked (shouted) me into trying my luck in a tournament some time ago and, to my astonishment, I won a medal. Admittedly, it was a bronze medal in a race where there were only three swimmers in the M40 category, but if someone wants to give me a medal for basically not being dead, I'm up for it. When I first started out I had the typical triathlete's view of swimming – no dives or tumble turns because you never do them in races, and every pool swim is merely a training opportunity so doing anything other than freestyle for anything less than 400m is pointless heresy. However, over time I realised that it's the other strokes where the medals are to be found, precisely because no other bugger does them. At my most recent Masters tournament I won SEVEN medals – three golds, two silvers and three bronzes – and only one was for freestyle. I even won one for individual medley, a vicious invention that sees you do all four strokes at once before spending the next ten minutes trying to get your heart rate back under 200. Now I don't mean to denigrate the athletic abilities of Masters swimmers, who frequently have bodies shaped like Dairylea triangles and can post times for 100m that I'd be hard pushed to match on a bike, it's just that there aren't many of them. The numbers get even fewer if you are female or over 40 – in fact come the day I'm a 73-year-old woman I'll be quids in. It's also worth noting that, although I've made it sound easy, there are lots of ways to get disqualified at swimming. You can choose from false start, screw-kick, not touching the wall with both hands, not turning properly, not handing your racecard in, and farting on the starting blocks – although that might just have been me. From the moment you step on to the blocks at the start you are alone and horribly exposed, and there are no opportunities for the usual triathlon open-water-mass-start skulduggery because the water is crystal clear and proceedings are watched over by more referees than – I don't know, I ran out of metaphors after the Mr T gag, from now on you're on your own.

As well as the obvious benefits of getting faster at swimming and winning a chest full of non-ferrous metals, there are lots of other plus-sides to Masters tournaments, not least that hanging round swimming pools all day is fantastic for your core strength because you spend hours holding your stomach in. The only downside to Masters events that I can think of is that they are uncomfortably like being back at school doing swimming galas, and in the changing room it's hard for me to repress the urge to flick my teammates' backsides with a wet towel or swing the metal clothes basket against the floor so it kicks up sparks. Actually no, there is another downside, which is that you are surrounded by swimmers, who have an uncomfortable habit of wanting to do lots of swimming. And it's for this reason I got talked into swimming the Channel...

It was all the fault of the fourth member of our Roth party, Muhammad McMenamin, who, one stormy night while we were both pissed, said, 'We should have a go at the Channel' to which I, of course, replied, 'Yes.' Because I'm a twat. I thought no more of it and dismissed it as the usual, inebriated nonsense triathletes come out with when they have sniffed the barmaid's apron, but little did I know that Steve, who is also a Masters swimmer, was serious. Before I knew it, he'd booked the pilot boats, registered us with the Channel Swimming and Piloting Federation, organised medical tests, ordered a vat of goose fat and sent me a white feather.

Swimming the Channel is the ultimate challenge in open water swimming, a pastime that has more than enough challenges associated with it. Ironmans all involve open water swimming in the sea, lakes and canals, with temperatures ranging from Baltic to Arctic. In fact, I think I'm beginning to suffer from a rare new medical condition – 'Open Water Tourettes.' The symptoms appear to be the sudden and violent urge to say the f-word repeatedly, whenever I dive into a lake for a training swim. This is usually to do with the coldness of the water and there's no denying I suffered a particularly bad case of OWT at the start of this season, when the British summer finally arrived with a 10-degree drop in temperature and two solid days of rain. Despite the confident declaration of the swim-marshals at the lake I was training in that the water temperature was '14 and rising', on diving into the lake I still exploded into a barrage of swear words that made Gordon Ramsay sound like Noddy. This was particularly unfortunate because there was a group of Cub Scouts watching and I don't think Akela was very pleased that his troop witnessed a blue-faced man shooting out of the water like a Polaris missile while shouting 'faaaaarrrrrrkkkkk' at the top of his voice. It's also worth mentioning that when I say 'dived into the lake', I'm stretching the definition of the word 'dive' a bit. The reality is that, like most of the Saturday swimmers at my local lake, I pick my way into the water like a clown crossing a minefield, before standing waist deep in the water for five minutes trying to summon up the courage to pitch forward into the icy wastes. I usually try to do this while staring off into the middle distance with hands on hips and jaw sticking out, trying to look tough and gritty just in case any girls from the Playboy mansion should happen to be passing.

Our training for the Channel swim mostly took place in Brighton where Steve lives and where there were indeed plenty of girls passing, normally on their way back from a hen night just as we were picking our way across the stones to the water's edge at 6.00 a.m. wearing nothing but Speedos and a look of terror. Conditions for swimming at Brighton are best described as 'borderline' (i.e. borderline psychopathic) with 7ft waves, driving rain and a howling wind all combining to make it about as pleasant as type 2 diabetes. Having been thrown about like a piece of flailing human jetsam for an hour the real fun came though when I tried to get out, with two waves smacking me so hard they ripped my goggles off and threw me headfirst into a kind of pebbly washing machine before I was spat out on to the beach. To complete our pleasure a large female lifeguard with everything a man could want (muscles and a moustache) was waiting for us with three key questions:

1. Did we see the red flags that forbade swimming that day?

2. Why didn't we tell them we were going to be swimming?

3. Did we know that we were 'causing distress to the public' who had seen us lolloping around in the water and assumed we were drunks who had fallen off the pier?

To which the answers obviously were:

1. Yes, but we pretended we hadn't.

2. Because you were still in bed when we plunged in at 6.00 a.m.

3. If you think that's bad wait 'til I take my trunks off.

So far you'll note that I've successfully implied to you that we were going to be swimming the Channel solo, whereas I've actually been bending the truth so far it's virtually a balloon animal. I was just one cog in a well-oiled machine of a team called 'The League Mentalmen', which was making a relay attempt to get to France without spending any money on ferries. And what a team it was! There was Steve 'Ice Man' Howes, Robin Corder and a bloke I hadn't met yet called Andy Heath, who I was counting on to be a relative of Michael Phelps. The Ice Man was so named because I've got more fat in my fingernails than he has in his whole body and he had been finding the sea temperature a bit on the nippy side. Lastly there was me, with my legs the size of a bookie's biro. How could we possibly fail?

But what of Steve Mac? Well, he had assembled a rival team that was taking the whole business far more seriously than us and was made up of biriyani-boy himself, Karen Throsby and Jamie Goodhead. As a Brighton resident, Steve was experienced in sea-swimming, making regular attempts to kill himself by swimming under Brighton Pier. Karen was doing the relay version first as a warm-up for having a go at a solo crossing, while Australian Jamie, having lived in the UK for too long, was trying to make a swim for it. All in all, they didn't stand a chance against us. Earlier on I cautioned you against getting involved with these open water swimming types, and here's why … Imagine it is 2.45 a.m., pitch dark, and you're on a small boat in the middle of the English Channel. You're standing on the back of the boat holding on to a ladder with your feet in the water, waiting for a klaxon to signal the moment at which you will jump into the sea. The water temperature is 16 degrees and you are wearing nothing but a pair of Speedos. Should you ever find yourself in this position, I can absolutely guarantee what you will be thinking, and it will be: 'WHAT AM I

DOING?!' This is certainly what went through my mind as I clung to the back of the good ship *Sea Satin*, waiting to take my turn on our relay swim.

Our team of four had been going for two hours, starting from Dover just after midnight. Big Andy did the first hour, Robin was just completing the second hour and I was the next in to bat. Both Andy and Robin swam well and looked comfortable, heaping pressure on me not to be crap. Inevitably the klaxon of death went and I jumped in. I was expecting it to be cold and we'd been told the water was a cool but manageable 16 degrees. The water I jumped into felt more like 1.6 degrees. It was so cold I couldn't swear. Or swim. Or breathe. I just made this gasping noise and started windmilling frantically to get round to the side of the boat where the spotlight was. I don't know if you have ever swum in the sea, in the dark, but take it from me, it isn't for the nervous-natured. I'm not usually afraid of the dark, but then I don't usually encounter quite so much of it. It was above me, ahead of me, behind me and, most importantly, underneath me. I am not afraid to say that I was absolutely cacking myself and I stuck to the spotlight beam like a moth. So began possibly the least pleasant hour of my life, which involved a freezing, pitch-black swim through the saltiest, most seaweed-blanketed water in the world, and I swam as though my life depended on it – which it did. After trying desperately to count the seconds and minutes that make up an hour, I was mightily relieved when a green flashing light on deck signalled that our fourth and final team member, Steve the Iceman, was readying himself for a watery grave. The klaxon went and I was on the boat faster than a Somali pirate.

Much had changed on the Good Ship Lollipop while I was paddling about. Andy was now gripped by seasickness and was retching at ten-second intervals, but I was too busy searching for a towel, dry clothes and some bravery before settling down on the poop deck for a snooze. I was dozing when a sharply worded exchange between ship's captain Lance and the Iceman awoke me:

| | |
|---|---|
| Captain Lance: | Are you all right, mate? |
| Steve the Iceman: | I want to get out. |
| Lance: | You can't, you've only done thirty minutes. |
| Iceman: | I'm cold. |
| Lance the pilot: | Well keep swimming then. |

Steve is not given to making such announcements lightly. He's done the Ironman world finals five times, won his age group at Ironman Austria, cycled from Land's End to John O'Groats and he's done a DOUBLE Ironman. In the Channel, though, he felt the cold more than the rest of us, due to having the same percentage body fat as a paperclip. However, showing true determination he dug in and finished his hour before coming aboard and amusing us all with an impersonation of a man getting changed during an earthquake as he tried to stop shivering long enough to put his pants on. The next four hours were a repeat of the first four except it was now light, which wasn't all it was cracked up to be because we could now see that we were in the shipping lanes with tankers and ferries all approaching at ramming speed. Seasick Andy did his turn before returning on board to resume his retch-athon and bobbin' Robin took over, clawing his way through impressive mountains of detergent foam dumped by passing container ships. My turn came and went in a flurry of thrashing arms and salty burping, before the Iceman returned to the frozen deep. After eight hours bobbing along in a sick bucket you'd think we would be starting to get a bit disheartened, or perhaps show the first signs of scurvy. However the third stint turned into our best. The sun came up, our speed went up and on my third hour something wonderful happened – France hove into view on the horizon.

The sight of the coast sparked renewed vigour and even the Iceman forgot his bone-shaking to put in a super-fast hour. There was, of course, another reason why we put on a sudden spurt for French waters. As I mentioned, we weren't just swimming across the Channel, we were *racing* across the Channel! Starting alongside us was the other boat, *Gallivant*. They had been close behind us from the word go and were now making an attempt to overtake. Seeing them trying to sneak up roused us to action and all of us put in some big turns, none more so than Seasick Andy who struck out for the coast like a man possessed (mostly so he didn't have to get back on the boat.) Despite the best efforts of the tides to take us off towards, variously, Belgium and Brazil, we all swam to the beach together, dragging ourselves on to the stony French shore in 12 hours 58 minutes. We remained on the beach for all of about three minutes before sprinting back to the boat and rushing over to where *Gallivant* was chugging along to have a hearty laugh as the 'swimmers' lugged themselves ashore twenty minutes behind us.

After a thoroughly enjoyable gloat our boat turned round, for a three-hour ride home to the merry sound of Andy retching.

As ever with these things, there's more to that Channel swimming lark than meets the eye. You can be the strongest swimmer in the world but time, tide, cold, shipping lanes, swell, wind, dark and fear are all there to stop you succeeding. The tides alone are not to be underestimated. As the crow flies it's just over 20 miles from England to France, but the tides meant we swam closer to 35 miles. However, the boat pilots are geniuses who know every inch of the ocean and who encourage you to reach certain points at certain times with ancient nautical phrases like 'get a fucking move on or we'll miss the tide.'

Back at the pool I have now finished this morning's session and am having a crafty wee in the pool as a parting gift for the members of the public who are waiting to get in at the end of the lane, hands on hips with impatience, like any of them are going to be any good. This is the point at which the professional triathletes would be whisked away by sedan chair back to their beds, or given a hearty breakfast of muesli or something else that looks like it's been swept out of a pigeon loft. For me, though, I now have to go straight to work. And how will I get there? Why I'll cycle of course.

# Chapter 4

Cycling probably dominates my life more than anything else. 'What's that, Martyn?!' you say. 'Surely you spend more time coming up with irritating ways to humiliate your friends more than anything else.' And perhaps you're right, having just got back from the airport to collect my friend and fellow triathlete Neill Morgan who has returned from his fortnight's holiday to Lanzarote. Neill is of a non-lofty stature and looks like a normal-sized person who's been hit by a lift, and was embarrassed but not surprised to be greeted by me at the airport standing among the ranks of taxi drivers holding up a big card with the word 'Hobbit' scrawled on it.

On balance, though, I'd say it was cycling because it dominates my work, my travel, my clothes, my holidays, my Sundays, most of my spare time, my medicine cabinet and the majority of my racing. I'm not sure what it is that leaves triathletes so much in thrall to cycling. When triathletes speak of triathlon, it is pretty much always cycling that dominates (when they aren't playing top-trumps over injuries, comparing excuses and exaggerating achievements). Triathletes always seem so much prouder of being good at cycling than of accomplishments in swimming or running and will happily spend ten times the amount of time training on it even though it's probably what they are already best at.

This may partly be down to the fact that, although

triathlons involve three sports, cycling accounts for about 50 per cent of the race time-wise. This is certainly the case with Ironmans, where you can easily be on the bike for five of the ten hours it takes you to finish (okay, okay, six of the 12 hours then). It's for this reason that I am frequently up at 5.00 a.m. disappearing out into the misty lanes on my bike with just the rabbits for company, embarking on a 100-plus mile ride that will take most of my Sunday. I could head out later but doing so has in the past incurred the wrath of my wife, Nicky, who may wish me to complete some sort of domestic chore or visit her parents, and she would prefer it if I was not late, reeking like an Arab drain, and falling asleep with my face in a Family Circle biscuit tin. It is similarly hard to visit any of my own elderly relatives on a Sunday afternoon because maintaining consciousness is hard when you are being regaled with fascinating views about how the world was so much nicer in the fifties. Back then, apparently, you could leave your doors unlocked, men doffed their caps to you and all the world's problems could be solved by a clip round the ear from a friendly policeman or, if that didn't work, hanging.

Most Sundays I'm up with the lark and out with the returning drunks to get a good training ride in, because the cycling leg of an Ironman is 112 miles long and not to be underestimated. My typical ride will involve doing about an hour on my own through the glorious mine-shafted countryside of north Warwickshire before rolling into a Coventry pub car park to meet up with my clubmates from Coventry Road Club. I've been a member of CRC for a few years now and each Sunday the massed ranks of Coventry's finest roadies assemble to do battle over a circuitous and friendly 50-or-so-mile ride into the countryside to a café, a convivial pot of tea and some baked beans on toast, before setting off home again trying to cut each other's throats by cranking up the pace to maximum, launching attacks and generally committing more acts of betrayal than Caligula. Once back at the pub car park, assuming I haven't been dropped or left puking in some roadside ditch, I will then ride another hour back through the lanes home before doing my best to convince a watchful Nicky that my droopy-eyed staggering does not mean that I am about to fall asleep, and that I am not about to suggest that I might leave her to go and visit her brother on her own, thus avoiding watching them engage in an afternoon of unsatisfying, snippy arguments.

'Club runs', as they are known, are a vital part of my training for Ironmans. Many triathletes train alone in the mistaken belief that as you have to ride alone during the race, you need to train alone to get used to it. However, this doesn't take account of the improved bike handling skills you get from riding with others, the pearls of wisdom about ways to save energy and ride efficiently that come from experienced cyclists, and the fact that they will spend a significant portion of the ride trying to drop you, leaving you pedalling alone in the middle of the countryside where they don't like outsiders, and where they don't bushwhack you like normal people in cities do but instead they shag you, and then eat you. There's certainly no better way to get faster on a bike than the prospect of being left behind by the group and I have gained strength and speed through chewing the bar-tape on my handlebars with the effort of trying to keep up. The club-runs at CRC usually divide into three – the family group that is heading out for 50 to 60 miles at a nice steady pace with the aim of keeping everyone together, the 'vets' group that will do about 60 to 75 miles at a slightly faster pace depending on who is out and will mostly stick together, and the 'training group' who will do 80 to 90 miles and will ride hard on the way out to the café before being scattered to the four winds on the way back when it's every man for himself and hang on if you can.

If I'm going well I'll head out with the training group, and if I'm feeling tired, lazy or a bit scared of the route we are doing that day, then I'll be lurking in the middle of the vets group hoping that my coach Dave Watson doesn't spot me and yell at me to get over there with the fast boys. Dave rides with the training group and is often the chief architect of cranking up the pace to the point where I'm sweating spinal fluid. Fair enough really, because he is an awesome cyclist who is a frequent winner of local road races and time trials, has ridden in the national road race and time trial championships having rubbed shoulders with Bradley Wiggins, Mark Cavendish et al, and can knock out 100 miles in less than four hours. He's been coaching me for about five years now and has been responsible for a massive improvement in my athletic abilities, mostly due to the fact that I fear him more than I fear death itself. Like all good coaches he is friendly and approachable, yet with the blank, dead-eyed stare of a mass murderer whenever you try to explain what went wrong in your race or why you didn't complete your training schedule.

As an example, me and my mate Phil Richmond, who was also coached by Dave, turned up to a weight training session once along with a third lad called Lee, a notorious training dodger. Dave, who was already there slamming a medicine ball around in an agitated state, fixed me with his Gestapo stare and said, 'What training have you done this week?' I stammered out all the things I had done that were on the plan he'd given me, as did Phil when it was his turn for the anglepoise lamp in the face. When it was Lee's turn, however, the real reason for this impromptu grilling emerged – Dave knew full well Lee hadn't trained and he watched silently while Lee lied through his soon-to-be-missing teeth. At this point Phil and I edged our way slowly back out of the room, bravely abandoning Lee to what was coming, and began our warm-up outside on the running track. We left it a safe period before returning to the gym and an atmosphere you could cut with a cricket stump. Dave was hefting a massive kettlebell in one corner, Lee was tearfully packing up his kit in the other and me and Phil, anxious not to provoke further ire, utterly ignored Lee when he slunk away never to be seen again. It was some minutes before Dave spoke, merely to offer the word 'Twat' before putting us all through the session from hell. Thanks, Lee.

Another area of my life that cycling dominates is my evenings because being coached by Dave has led to me taking up time trials. If you are unfamiliar with what time trials are then let me enlighten you. TTs are basically bike races against the clock that take place most spring and summer weekday evenings across the UK. Although principally for cyclists, a growing number of triathletes have started taking them up because of the many training benefits that can be gained from being hunched over a low-pro bike on a blustery dual carriageway while adopting an expression that looks like a frowny face someone has drawn on to their scrotum. Time trials used to be the preserve of monosyllabic old men with knees that looked like haggis made of knuckles, who would nevertheless come flying past you once the race started. These days, however, time trials are the second most popular activity in lay-bys across the country, and innocent triathletes are constantly trying to decipher course codes and entry forms that look as though they can only be solved with an Enigma machine. For example the K10/10K, to use an example local to me, is a code for a particular ten mile course that harks back to a time when time triallists had to hide their illegal racing activities from the police lest they be given a clip round the ear by the local bobby or, for courses near London, kettled and then shot. Time trials are very different from triathlons in a number of ways:

- There is no inflatable finish line with crowds of adoring fans, a photographer and an energy drink. If you're lucky you might get a chequered bit of wood and a windswept old bloke who looks like a campaign poster for neglected horses, who will sternly note down your time on a clipboard and then offer you a fondant fancy and a cup of tea so stewed it will strip the skin off your gums.

- The entry form is more complicated than a travel permit from the Stasi and demands that you not only remember all your previous results over various distances to the exact second, but the winner's exact results, too. This is so you can be seeded to prevent drafting behind another cyclist, which of course never, ever happens in triathlons.

- On the plus side they only cost a couple of quid to enter and you don't pay a fortune for a bag full of advertising crap.

- No matter how fast you think you are, there will be several people there who will finish in times that you cannot comprehend. This has been particularly the case during the recent economic downturn because, as one wise old cyclist told me, you can always tell when there's a recession on – the pace of races gets faster thanks to people having more time off to go training.

- There seems to be a particular type of storm front called cumulo-timetrialus, which lurks invisible to the naked eye until the moment I reach the start line of a time trial, whereupon it races overhead and dumps the equivalent of Rutland Water on me. This has happened to me twice recently, with the most recent downpour a particularly biblical affair as I took part in the Heanor Clarion CC 25 miler at Ettwall in Derbyshire. Despite spray from passing lorries, lashing rain, standing water and slippery roundabouts I broke the hour (58.08 ithankyew) thanks to a strong desire to get away from the lorries on the A50 as fast as humanly possible. I was very pleased to be a) under the hour and b) alive, and – a quick word to any local councils reading this – these so called 'speed-bumps' you build are rubbish. If anything, they slow you down.

Yet further evidence that cycling dominates my life is that it now accounts for at least two holidays I take every year. Obviously there's the holiday abroad to take part in Ironman races, so this year lucky Nicky is being treated to a break on the sun-kissed shores of southern Bavaria. However, for the past few springs, the unsightly, malodorous perverts that constitute my friends and I have also headed out to Majorca to make up for three months of dossing about by cycling 450 miles in six days. During spring Majorca is a mecca for road cyclists who swarm all over the island like the Ebola virus, in search of ice-free roads and contaminated beef. The effects of going from training-dodger to pro-cyclist overnight could easily be replicated by staying at home and smashing myself repeatedly on the quads with a rolling pin, but if I just did that I wouldn't be able to tell my non-triathlete neighbours that I was away at a 'training camp', thus fooling them into believing that I'm a serious athlete with talent and prospects. This annual pilgrimage to the mountains and cake shops of Spain's version of the Isle of Wight follows a fairly typical pattern that involves my mates and me trying to drop each other on the climbs, trying to drop each other on the flat, trying to drop groups of German cyclists that we've just hammered past, and committing acts of foul treachery to win sprints for village signs. My alternative training camp destination is Snowdonia on trips organised by coach Dave. I have spent many dripping weekends slogging my way round enough vertical roads and vowel-free villages in mid Wales to make even the most ardent Plaid Cymru freedom fighter want to piss off to the sunshine for a bit.

Now that I've been attending these Majorcan sojourns for a few years, there's something about training camps that has always mystified me – which is that people train to go on them. I've always viewed them as a way of dragging myself into some sort of shape, so I'm happy to turn up with my winter belly and creaky legs and set about huffing and puffing my way to fitness. Not so everyone else, who arrives having cycled, swum and run their way into tip top form over the past few weeks and set about beating me up in every session. Not that I don't do any preparation at all for this trip. Indeed, for the few weeks before I go, I give my own spin to the tapas and a glass of salty manzanilla on the terrace by sitting in the park with a bag of Tangy Toms and a bottle of Harvey's Bristol Cream. Olé! Also, like all committed employees, in the weeks before I head sunwards I'm busy covering my back, besmirching other colleagues and shredding the evidence of my incompetence.

Our rides around the island usually take us from Port de Pollenca along the coast to Zita corner, across the Bullrush Road, up the Col de Steps, down the Col de Walls, over the Schnell Bridge, past Smithy's Hole and down the Rue de Two Dogs Shagging. Studying maps will reveal none of these place names (apart from Port de

Pollenca), because they are coded references to incidents that have occurred over the years. The Schnell Bridge for example is so named because as we approached it once we bore down on a group of German cyclists in front. As we reeled them in over the bridge the rider at the back was heard to shout up to the front 'Schnell! Schnell! Das Englanders!', which almost caused our group leader Richard 'Todger' Todd to fall off laughing. Smithy's Hole is named simply after a pothole hit at full pelt by Dave Smith, one of our number. While soaring airborne over his handlebars he looked like the most majestically graceful turkey you can imagine before he hit the deck with an audible splat.

Aerial dogfight re-enactments aside, it's a great place to go and get some warm weather training done and while Egypt and Syria offer cheaper deals, it's less noisy in Majorca and the natives seem friendlier. That said, I've never been there in summer when the vandal hordes of British tourists arrive. Let's hope they never start rioting because it would be useless firing tear gas at someone who smokes sixty Lambert and Butler a day.

Training abroad also means you have the added satisfaction of knowing that everyone at home will be freezing their tits off and hates your guts every time you text them to tell them the local temperature and your daily mileage. I've always had to tread somewhat carefully with the lads I go to Majorca with like Todger and Andrew 'Peachy' Waters-Peach, a massively powerful time-triallist and huffing swimmer, because they are hardened cyclists and in this company I have always been viewed as something of a novelty. Being a triathlete means I am the only one to get back to the hotel after a day's hard cycling, leap (slump) off my bike, don my trainers and head straight off for a bandy-legged two-hour shuffle. Mostly I was eyed with contempt by the cyclists, although they warmed to me after the occasion when my foot slipped out of the pedal as I dismounted and my bike's top tube smacked me straight in the clinkers, leaving me to spend the rest of the day talking like Joe Pasquale. I am delighted to say, though, that I am now no longer alone, and the number of compression socks on cyclists, coupled with the number of wetsuits hanging on hotel balconies and the number of skinsuits and sun-visors seen plodding along beachfront roads in the midday sun, all indicate that the triathlete population is gradually taking over, forcing the cyclists out to the fringes. This may be thanks to Ironman Mallorca, which launched a few years ago. Whenever I go these days there are more people than ever out riding the racecourse and dicing with death by hurtling down Selva Gorge on their tri-bars. Happily the triathletes seem to have assimilated with the cyclists by observing the golden rules of training camps:

1. Always turn up at training camp saying you haven't trained. Then try to duff everyone else up in the first session.

2. Always carefully select which race T-shirt to wear at breakfast so you can pose in front of your fellow continental buffet diners showing what you have achieved.

3. When bearing down on German cyclists, never 'sit in' behind them but instead attack and overtake at the first opportunity while maintaining a facial expression that suggests you are not trying.

4. The only Spanish phrase you should speak all week is 'café con leche por favor.'

5. Always undo six days of Trappist monk-like living and avoiding anything deep fried at the buffet by getting out of your face on bargain lager on the final night and quickly resuming a potato-based lifestyle.

6. Have absolutely nothing to do with any non-athletic holidaymakers who are there at the same time, who look like a bunch of Wookies dressed by Primark, and often possess a backside so big you could crucify someone on it.

Cycling in the sunshine on quiet Majorcan roads is one thing, but if you want to be any good at it then inevitably you'll have to do some of it in the winter in the UK as well, which is, of course, all-year-round fun – and I use the word 'fun' quite wrongly. Training in the winter is a necessary evil. By that I mean it is vaguely necessary but definitely evil. Being a triathlete in winter is hard enough anyway because one side of your brain says that as well as the season to be jolly, 'tis also the season of rest, recovery, cakes and long-postponed nights in the pub. You've trained hard, raced hard, eaten healthily, shunned alcohol and you bloody well deserve a rest. Except the other part of your brain nags you with thoughts that every pint, biscuit, Belgian chocolate and individual mince pie is weighing you down, making you slow and rubbish. You'll be overweight in a week, next season everyone will beat you and your results will plummet faster than a fat kid off a 10-metre diving board. So we keep training.

In the UK, training in the winter isn't that different from training in the summer except the days are shorter and you have to clean more crap off your bike, but there's only so much rain a cyclist can take before their feet become webbed so there comes a point when we are driven indoors. Fiendish minds have been at work and have devised a glittering array of fun-packed ways to ensure you stay at it no matter what the weather.

Firstly there are turbo trainers, which began life as an instrument of torture with the first recorded use being during the Spanish Inquisition, when confessions were extracted from heretics by attempting to sweat them to death. Now adapted as a training 'aid', they sap your legs and your soul by clamping your back wheel into a static metal frame, pushing a magnetic roller against your tyre and allowing you to pedal while sitting still, giving you all the effort of cycling outside but without some of the pleasanter aspects such as air to breathe, a view to see, and blood to circulate around your groin. My turbo trainer sits in the garage staring malevolently at me as the nights draw in. I am convinced it is evil because I once cut myself on a tyre lever and my blood seemed to flow towards it. Soon it will have my rear wheel in its vice-like grip, and it knows it. Hour upon hour of crotch-numbing pedalling awaits.

Turbo trainers are not the only means of indoor cycling torture. Oh no, there are spinning classes, which are the fitness equivalent of Chris Evans in that they shout fun but they feel shit. They typically involve thunderous pedalling to pumping music which is so bad that if it came on the radio while I was in my car, I couldn't kick the knob off the stereo fast enough. The music does at least have the blessing of drowning out the excited whoops of the spinning instructor exhorting us to 'feel the burn' while I am wishing they could feel the lash of a bicycle chain. The other downside to spinning classes is that they tend to be attended by non-cyclists who are just there to keep fit (or get fit judging by the look of some of them). While training for Ironman Canada I did a deal with the Esporta gym opposite where I worked at that time, that I could go in and join their spinning classes while training for the race. I duly turned up and plonked myself on a bike in the middle of the studio and started warming up. Around me were several people, mostly women of a certain age and wealth, wearing pristine Nike kit with attendant accessories such as headbands, drinks bottles and make-up. Most were pedalling slowly and chatting away while the excitable female instructor started cranking up the music and hormones. I did as I was bid, and started powering away, sweating like a piece of cheese under Anthony Worrall Thompson's jacket and spraying perspiration around like a garden hose. After a few minutes of this I glanced up to see that I was now surrounded by a ring of empty bikes, the cast of *Loose Women* having moved to the fringes of the studio to avoid that awful man whose skin appeared to be leaking.

It is worth mentioning at this point that you can also train indoors for other parts of triathlon. In running you can try a treadmill, which is a bit like a turbo trainer except that it has the extra comedy potential that you might see someone trip over and get fired out the back like they've been shot from a catapult. Then there's circuit training, which involves running round a room doing press-ups, squat thrusts, box-jumps, burpees, reverse dips, pull-ups, sit-ups and 'Oh, God my stomach hurts and my arms are going to drop off and I think I'm going to diiiiieeeeee!' If you are really committed you could also try weight training, which involves hanging around in strange rooms where scantily clad people spend a lot of time looking at themselves in mirrors and making the kind of loud straining noises you only otherwise hear in the toilets at motorway services. Being able to lift enormous weights is less important than being world class at posing around while inadequately clad, and I don't find going to the gym a comfortable experience. To be honest I'm a bit clueless about it all. For example, the push-up bra I bought recently is hopeless. Even when I'm wearing it I can still only do about ten of them.

So far we've discussed how cycling dominates my free time in the winter and summer, but it dominates my working life, too. Partly this is because these days I don't own a car, just a campervan that is capable of passing everything on the road except a petrol station, so consequently I cycle everywhere as my main mode of transport. It is also partly because I now have a job in cycling, which came about as a direct result of me taking up triathlons. Let me explain …

If you've ever heard of me before, it's probably because you have read a column I write in a monthly magazine called *220 Triathlon* (the 220 being the number of people who read my column, timesed by ten), an opportunity that came my way after winning a readers' competition to see how many knob gags one person could fit into a single paragraph. Despite appearances I am not a professional writer – which you may well have worked out for yourself if you're still with me this far into the book – and I've had several jobs in what I laughingly call 'my career' so far, all of them crap. However, these days to keep a roof over my pretty little head I have a job that involves helping to convert old railway lines into cycle routes, and travelling round the country identifying places where new cycle paths and bridges can be built. This obviously sounds like a lot of fun – and it is, I won't lie. The organisation I work for is a charity called Sustrans, which is responsible for creating the 14,000 miles of the National Cycle Network, and as its development manager I spend most of my days on a bike, riding around looking at places where cyclists have a hard time as a result of the design of roads and speeds of traffic, trying to see what can be done about it. Admittedly, I'm usually riding round on a Brompton folding bike that makes me a figure of fun to schoolkids and the occasional commuter on the trains I catch but, as I recently pointed out to one gentleman with a face like a dog's bum with a hat on who suggested that my 6 foot 3 inch frame perched on top of a mini-wheeled roller skate made me look like 'a twat', in my world it wasn't as hopelessly twattish as wearing an ill-fitting Marks & Spencer suit on a train with 300 identically dressed people who all wish they were doing something else other than spending 40 hours of misery a week in a corporate shitfarm.

Going to work for Sustrans was a complete departure from the previous jobs I'd had, which all involved working in 'head office' type roles for large corporations, doing things so pointless that if I tried to explain them you'd be asleep before I reached the end of the sentence. A great test of this is whether or not you can explain what you do for a living to your mum. Mind you, based on what she's heard from me, my mum thinks triathlons basically involve cycling around in a leotard, shitting in hedges. However, something happened to me while I was training for Ironman Lake Placid a few years ago that changed all this, which is that I got banned from driving. I'm at pains to point out that I was not banned for drink-driving or insane speeding, but under the totting-up rules that come with regularly acquiring three points on your licence thanks to driving through speed cameras at 5–10mph over the speed limit. The camera that did for me was in Melton Mowbray, which I was only passing through because I was off to do a triathlon at Rutland Water called The Vitruvian. It was about 4.00 a.m. and I was peering for road signs when a flash alerted me to the fact that the speed limit had just dropped from 40mph to 30, and with 11 points already to my name, I'd just fucked my driving licence into a cocked hat. I subsequently had to appear at Melton magistrates court and stand before three very stern looking public servants who pronounced the death sentence until reminded that this wasn't an option any more. I hoped that transportation to Australia would be next, but instead I got a six month suspension and told that if I drove during that six months I could go to prison. My prosecutors did not look amused when I said, 'I thought all the prisons were full' and it was with their dire warnings ringing in my ears that I subsequently drove all the way back to Coventry …

Fair dos, though I didn't drive after that and I have no complaints because I deserved it, having driven like an arse for many a moon. Not one to have his stride broken, I took this as an opportunity to do some extra cycle training by riding to work every day. What I hadn't considered, though, was that commuting by bike through towns during rush hour is very different to Sunday morning training in country lanes, and the roads these days are just about safer now than in the Middle Ages when we slept on straw and were regularly attacked by marauders. The longer I went on cycling every day, the more I realised how bad it could be trying to get around on a bike thanks to the way roads were designed and the way some drivers behaved, and the more I resolved to do something about it. Consequently when my six months' ban was up three important things happened:

1. I didn't bother getting another car because despite the difficulties with cycle commuting, I was better off and less stressed than when I had a car, and if anything was getting to places earlier.

2. I decided to leave my job and get one that tried to improve the lot of cyclists in the UK.

3.  I ended up spending a fortune on chafe cream and Anusol to get rid of the bad case of arse-biscuits (those small but painful lumps that appear on your chuff) I'd acquired through cycling every day.

So when I say cycling rules my life more than anything else, it's probably true because it accounts for work time, playtime, commuting time, training time and toilet time. I now have seven bikes in my garage, each with a specific purpose – road racing, triathlons and time trials, commuting, mountain biking, winter training, turbo-ing and unfolding so I can perch on top of it to be mocked by schoolchildren. I'm not ashamed of having this many bikes, in fact I'm quite proud of it, and my only real fear is that one day my wife will sell them for the amount of money I told her that I'd paid for them …

# Chapter 5

I am currently typing while sat at my dining room table wearing nothing but a pair of split-sided running shorts, long compression socks and nipple tape – and if that mental image doesn't put you in the mood for romance, nothing will. The reason for this singular look is that I have just returned from training with my running club, and the stench emanating from me is enough to drive away even my usually loyal Welsh Springer Spaniel Freddie, a creature frequently to be found with his nose up his own arsehole.

Running training kills me. Tonight's session was two one-mile laps out on the road at 5.45-a-mile pace, followed by eight times around the 400m track at 80 seconds per lap, before going back out on the road to repeat the two miles at 5.45 pace. Of course, what this turned into was the first mile at 5.30 pace, the second at 6 minute pace, then the eight 400s at a pace progressing (regressing) from 72 seconds up to 85, before going back out on the road to run another mile at 5.59 pace and the last at about 7 minute pace, by which point I am running like I've tipped a bag of crisps down my bum-crack. To make matters worse I am doing this session with my running club Coventry Godiva Harriers. Godiva, as it shall henceforth be known, is the real deal when it comes to running clubs, with a wall in the clubhouse covered in photos of club members who have been Olympians.

My running companions tonight included my friends Emerson Combstock, Pete Banks and Noel Edwards who have all represented England at distance running, Iwan Jones who has represented Wales, Zara Hyde-Peters who has run for Great Britain and Ian Gower who looks like he comes from the same planet as the Klingons.

The wider training group contains people who have won marathons, cross country races and various national championships, others who represent their counties, and several youngsters on the cusp of breaking into the international teams for European and Commonwealth games. To make matters yet more intimidating, this training session is being watched over by Dave Moorcroft (Commonwealth gold medallist, Olympian and former 5,000m world record holder), Colin Kirkham (ran the marathon for Great Britain in the 1972 Olympics) and Bill Adcocks (ran the marathon for Great Britain in the 1968 Olympics and broke the course record for the classic Athens marathon course, which he subsequently held for 30 years). And then there's me, huffing along at the back like an overweight stalker – and despite my angular physique, in this company I look distinctly overweight. The session is presided over by running coach Mike Peters, himself a sub 2.30 marathon runner and Stuart Pearce lookalike whose training sessions are guaranteed to turn me into a gastropod, in that by the end I am slow-moving with a slimy sheen.

Being able to run a long way without turning into a human daddy-long-legs is a vital part of training for an Ironman, so training sessions such as the one I have just endured must be completed if I am to have a hope in Roth. I put myself through this torture about three times a week, one consequence of which is that, thanks to my massive capacity for sweating, my kitbag now smells worse than a wrestler's loincloth and nothing I do can shift the stench. I even tried spraying it with Nicky's perfume but all that happened was a sailor followed me home. Running with this bunch is a far cry from where I started back in 2002. As I mentioned earlier, neither of the schools I went to were big on athletics, my junior school because anything other than football might as well have been pressing wild flowers and stamp collecting, and my senior school because only team games could turn you into the kind of upstanding member of the community that would make the school proud – solo sports were the preserve of loners and tomorrow's book depository gunmen. Consequently, I did not grow up having much to do with the athletic world and missed out on the halcyon days of the sport when boys raced boys, girls raced girls, and horses raced through your digestive system. This is a shame because in international terms this was a golden era for British athletes with Steve Ovett, Seb Coe, Alan Wells, Daley Thompson, Tessa Sanderson, Steve Cram, Brendan Foster, Peter Elliot and Fatima Whitbread all achieving world class success and, in the case of Fatima Whitbread, some top quality schoolboy jokes.

I used to love watching Daley Thompson and Steve Ovett in particular – Daley because he was the greatest ever, and Ovett because I much preferred him to Seb Coe on account of his apparent unpopularity with the media. Identifying with the anti-hero is something I've done my whole life, which is why I have the friends I have, I suppose. Despite being interested in athletics, this didn't translate into me actually getting off my arse and doing anything about it. It wasn't until I was 35 that I entered my first ever race. At that time I was working for Lord Vader of the Empire, also known as Barclays Bank, and in a bid to make ourselves feel that our working lives were even vaguely worthwhile, a bunch of us decided we'd go and do the Great North Run for charity. At this particular point in my life I was suffering from a medical condition known as being a 'fat bastard', tipping the scales at an impressive 15 stone, but still looking good – for someone twice my age. I wasn't particularly conscious of having got overweight and I didn't achieve it by anything as remarkable as a junk-food diet. I just steadily ballooned over a period of about 15 years until, by the time I was in my mid-thirties, I had achieved a waist size of 38 inches and I couldn't walk along any beach without fear of feeling the thump of a harpoon in my thorax from a passing Norwegian whaling ship.

In truth I probably thought I could do with losing a bit of weight and the Great North Run gave me a mission, a vision, a target, an impetus and lots of other wanky-banky phrases we were indoctrinated with at that time. My favourite was a poster on the office wall of a soaring bird of prey with the title 'Good Managers are like Eagles' – which was true, because you wouldn't have found either of them in that office. I set about training for the run by making my first mistake and joining my local gym, a costly place that was harder to leave than the Freemasons. However, they had treadmills aplenty and big screens showing Jamelia and Pussycat Dolls to distract me. I then went and bought a pair of trainers from JJB Sports (my second mistake) and began my self-created training plan – mistake number three. When I started I could literally run on a treadmill for five minutes before I had to stop, and with my ponderous pace and slowly undulating flesh I looked like a human lava lamp. However, the next time I went I ran for six minutes, then seven, then eight until after a while I was all the way up to an hour. I don't remember what my pace was, or even considering that such a thing as pace existed, but I don't recall ever considering running outside at any point, or doing longer than an hour, which was the maximum time setting on the treadmill.

When it came to doing the Great North Run, we all arrived at the start line in Newcastle at the same time as 40,000 other people, and I committed a sin that would come to enrage me in the future when others did it – I went down to the front of the race. My logic for this was that with the channel of competitors stretching back half a mile I'd end up going through the wall twice just to cross the start line. It never occurred to me that I would be getting in the way of lots of others, and indeed for the first mile I didn't because, committing mistake number four, I went off at the same pace as everyone around me. A slight tightening in my legs, chest, forehead, groin muscles and teeth told me after a couple of miles that I had gone off too fast and what followed was a kind of slap-footed shuffle through Tyneside while being quite rightly jostled by people trying to get round my girth. Despite the abominable preparation and poorly executed race strategy, I somehow contrived to cross the line in Gateshead in 1 hour and 59 minutes. This came as a revelation not just to me but also to my wife, who wasn't expecting me for another hour and who memorably said, 'What are you doing here, did you pack in?' My debut running time, coupled with having beaten all the other Barclays runners, convinced me that THIS was the sport I had been searching for all my life, that I was obviously a natural and that the world of running now consisted of me, Haile Gebrselassie and Paula Radcliffe in that order – mistake number five.

There are any number of sensible moves I could have made at this point, such as joining a running club, trying another half marathon or perhaps something shorter, or going to a proper running shop and getting some proper shoes rather than ones sold by some grunting teenaged host-organism for acne because 'they've got big heels innit.' My actual next move was to enter the London Marathon. The year was 2003, notable for the triple tragedies of the invasion of Iraq, the death of comic genius Bob Monkhouse, and the opening of Birmingham's Bullring shopping centre. It was not notable for an unheard-of runner shocking the world by winning the London Marathon in a pair of shitty old trainers. Quite why I thought doing a marathon was a good idea is lost in the mists of time; however I do recall a couple of things about my pre-race preparation:

1. I bought a new T-shirt.

2. I did absolutely no training for it whatsoever. And I mean that. None. Nothing. Not even the treadmill running I did for the Great North Run.

Ignorance is bliss, of course, and I don't remember being unduly concerned as I set off from Greenwich Park. Once again, I set off too fast, although partly this was to get away from a bloke calling himself the Karaoke Runner who had hooked up speakers to his belt and was running with microphone in hand, singing along to 'Keep on Running', 'Run to You', 'Everybody Wants to Run the World' and 'Corpses' by Ian Brown. Although that last one may have been what I was on the verge of turning him into. Despite my catastrophic lack of preparation my confidence was sky-high when I crossed the halfway point at Tower Bridge in 1 hour and 59 minutes, emulating my Gateshead time and underlining my latent potential as a running Gladiator. What followed was a series of episodes that meant that should I ever actually be selected to appear on *Gladiators*, my Gladiator name would have to be something like 'Blister', or 'Guff', or perhaps 'Spasm', 'Dunce', 'Void', 'Simpleton' or most accurately of all, 'Shitclown'.

First off, I started to feel a bit tired and my knees started to hurt. Then, without being conscious of the fact that I was slowing down, I was overtaken by a man dressed as a fairy who tapped his wand on my head as he skipped past. Then I was overtaken by an old woman who saw me shuffling along as though I'd soiled myself and said 'Repeat after me, this is fun', the vicious old cow. Next I was overtaken by a man dressed in a giant port bottle, two runners dressed as rhinos, and someone in a Mr Tickle costume. And then I heard it, 'Ohhhhhh, I'm going to run to you, yeeeeeah I'm going to run to you' as the Karaoke Runner came oozing up behind me. I searched for a chair leg or piece of broken pipe with which to kill myself, but instead opted for something more shameful – I walked. Anyone who has ever done this knows that once you stop running, starting again is almost impossible, and even greats like Paula Radcliffe struggle to get going once they've stopped staggering around a gutter in their knickers like a Greek holidaymaker.

Luckily though, after walking for a couple of miles (five) I spotted a man up ahead of me in the wide, sky blue, vertical stripes of a Coventry City shirt. If only I could catch him up we could talk football and distract ourselves from the misery and pain. It took me two miles to hunt him down when, to my shattering dismay, it turned out he was wearing an Argentina shirt! I don't remember much about the last few miles apart from crossing the finish line next to a lad I thought was quite fat but who, on the photos, looks the same size as me. Looking at the photos now I realise that I have carefully cut off the part of the gantry that shows my finishing time so people would never see it, but I'm now happy to reveal to all three of you who have bought this book that my finishing time was 5 hours 20 minutes, and despite my dreams of running greatness it had taken me almost three and a half hours to do the second half of the race. Reality is a bitch.

Skip forward ten years and, thanks to running with Godiva, things have changed somewhat. As contrasting evidence to my London experience I offer the experience of my last marathon, which took place around the attractive business parks and industrial estates of Abingdon in Oxfordshire, and for which I trained by temporarily abandoning any swimming, cycling or triathlon activity of any kind. If you are a triathlete then I realise this admission will probably make your tempers hotter than Peter Stringfellow's hairdryer, because the universal law of triathlon states that running should *never* be engaged in as a stand-alone activity, because that is wimpish. Triathlon is a multi-sport full of danger and gadgets, and for triathletes 5ks are 'a leg stretch', 10ks and half marathons don't count unless you cycle to them, and marathons should only be completed as a 'training session' for an Ironman. I broke this golden rule to concentrate on training for a marathon in a bid to complete one under the magic 3-hour barrier. I'd managed this once before a few years previously but rumours abounded that I was now past it, having done my previous two marathons in lovely Stockholm and not-so-lovely Leicester in 3.05 and 3.08. I decided that if I wanted to enhance my image as an athletic egotist wedged so tightly up my own sphincter that I'm basically just a burly haemorrhoid, then I needed to have a marathon result that started with a '2', proving that my last one wasn't a fluke. Also I needed something – anything! – to distract me from the fact that, at the time of this race, the triathlon season had finished and it was either run a marathon or spend the next few weeks pinned to my mattress by an invisible goblin of woe.

I chose the Abingdon Marathon as the scene of my shameful exploit because, like Challenge Roth, it is renowned as a 'fast' course, and I began doing some running – lots and lots of running. As far as my triathlon friends were concerned, news that I was 'just running' was treason that should be repaid with death, and I was told to either pledge loyalty to the God of Triathlon and live out my days as a wealthy lord with rich lands and many sons, or they'd have my head on a stick. However, by this time I'd begun my training plan set for me by Dave-who-shall-be-obeyed so it was too late to turn back. Training enables greater effort, harder sessions, and the need for more and more kit ... in other words, it enables most of the shit in my life. Without specific training I can categorically state I would never make it as a runner, because it just hurts too much. No freewheeling on your bike, no using your arms to give your legs a rest, no having a crafty rest in transitions, just hours and hours of endless effort that gives your legs the same flexibility as a two-pin plug.

Marathon runners in particular seem to me to be a strange, solitary breed who list their hobbies as things like 'training', 'cold baths' and 'preparing for the war against the machines', so it came as a relief that on marathon race day there were evidently plenty of triathletes doing the race, easily identified by their headsweats, caps, skinshorts, compression socks, special belt for holding gels and the latest-shiny-gadget on their wrists. They did not, however, identify me, because such was the extent to which I'd turned my back on triathlon that I wore just a vest and a pair of running shorts and I carried my gels in my hands rather than in some kind of specially designed belt – shameful stuff. The race itself was flat and twisty and when I set off at my 6.45-a-mile pace, half the field swarmed past me in a way that suggested that either

a)  I was still poor at running

or

b) half the field was over-optimistic about their fitness and repeating the mistake I made in Newcastle all those years ago.

The chief incidents of note during the race were a stabbing pain in my groin that made me consider changing my name to Screaming Lord Crutch, and duelling for five miles against a baldy runner with ill-fitting dentures who looked like Nosferatu, only much more real. On the plus side, at least he wasn't singing. I finally shook off Mr Baby-New-Potato-Head at mile 15, by which time I was steadily making my way back through the over-optimistic portion of the field who'd started too fast. At mile 18, I had an energy gel that tasted like Gollum dung and spent two miles gagging on vile glop but by mile 21 I was striding forth at 6.30-a-mile pace and waiting for 'The Wall' to rear up and smack me in the Jacob's cream crackers. The Wall, of course, is that infamous imaginary barrier that comes somewhere between 17 and 22 miles and which makes you stumble about like you've been for a night on the ale with Sarah Harding. Yet on this day The Wall never came despite 26.2 miles being a long way and me having the same bandy-legged gait by the end of the race as someone who had spent their life working on the waltzers. At the finish line I was so thin I had to eat five Curly-Wurlies before I became visible to the human eye and, despite being desperate for a pint, I was offered only a cup of tea by a marshal so young he couldn't have understood the phrase 'Give me Guinness' if I'd spelled it out with Sticklebricks. All this fandango was worth it because of the time as I crossed the line – 2.54:26. Boom-shakalaka-boom-shakalakalaka. Boom. That time is exactly 2 hours and 26 minutes faster than my first marathon. My Godiva teammates Emerson and Iwan would have time to go round the whole course again and still finish ahead of my fat former self, but not any more!

These days I've even managed to win a couple of medals for running (albeit 'Masters' medals, which are awarded to older runners who have defied death long enough to still be competing) and it is the part of triathlon that has had the most dramatic effect on my physique. I'm grateful for that because it's a good bit cheaper than paying someone to follow me round slapping pork pies out of my hand. On reflection, though, as Messrs Constable & Robinson publishers are paying me to be reflective, if there's one sport that has landed me in more trouble than any other, it is running.

## Trouble number one

One night a couple of years ago, after sliding home from the village pub, I went online and entered the Stockholm Marathon. I'd read an article about it earlier that day, saw a photo of a drinks station that appeared to be staffed entirely by Miss Sweden contestants in wet T-shirts and thought 'that's the race for me.' As I entered the race, the date rang a distant bell but, being pissed, I didn't dwell on it any further. It wasn't until the following day when Nicky asked me where we were going to go for her birthday that an icy claw gripped my insides and I was transformed from carefree triathlete into a dead-eyed totem of misery. Yes, the date of the marathon was indeed her birthday, and not just any old birthday but a landmark birthday, too. As this is a book that may be read at some point by somebody, let's say it was her twenty-first birthday, and definitely not her fortieth.

This was the point at which I should have said to Nicky, 'I have inadvertently entered the Stockholm Marathon while under the influence of Stella Artois, so how would you like a weekend there?' but, given that she has the compassion of a water cannon operator, instead I crapped my packet and squeaked, 'How would you like to go to Stockholm?' Her response was to get very excited, text all her friends to tell them she was off to the home of Ikea and their so-called chairs, and to cook me meatballs for tea. Her excitement reached fever pitch when she found out it was the same weekend as a Swedish royal wedding culminating in the 'Love Stockholm' festival, a three-day free booze, food and music jamboree. This was the point at which I should have said, 'Yes, and there's a marathon, too, which I'd really like to do, please may I enter it?' but once again, like a white mouse, I said nothing. I carried on saying nothing until we were boarding the flight to Arlanda Airport, at which point I thought the presence of armed security staff might make it the perfect moment to own up, given that she couldn't attack me without being subjected to gunfire.

She was already disappointed that her promised 'bottle of bubbly' was a half-used bottle of limited edition Matey from 1999, so as she asked what we were going to do on her birthday I said, 'Well, er, I wondered if you could spare me for a couple of hours …' Nicky gave me a look made entirely of ice and said, 'Why?'

'Well, there's a marathon which I may have already entered,' I replied, while experiencing more hot and cold flushes than a malaria patient going through the menopause. Nicky's face darkened and some birds flying overhead suddenly dropped dead out of the sky. In a flash, she understood precisely what had happened and that her birthday treat was little more than elaborate window dressing for another race. Then, instead of kicking my knees so hard that they folded the wrong way, she merely said, 'You'll pay for this' in a voice that suggested I would shortly be pecked to death by ravens. And I did pay for it, with expensive meals every night during which Nicky made me watch as she ate chips the size and weight of piano keys while I had to have salad and muesli. Her greatest revenge came within 20 minutes of me crossing the finish line of the race, whereupon she marched into the warm-down area where I was warming down by lying on the floor groaning and announced, 'Right, that's done. Now it's sightseeing time.' I spent the next three hours walking around every monument, park, festival event and shop in Stockholm, despite the fact that I couldn't have looked more uncomfortable if I'd been gelding a horse. I'd like to say there is a profound moral to this story but other than 'don't take your wife to races' I can't think what it might be.

**Trouble number two**
In 2009 I tore a muscle in my foot. This was particularly annoying because:

1. It hurt.

2. It was two weeks before I was due to run in the Stratford-upon-Avon marathon, a key part of my build-up for doing that year's Ironman Austria.

As it was, I showed great maturity at not being able to run in the marathon by going cycling for four hours in the opposite direction on race day and refusing to talk to any of my mates about their various personal bests (PBs) on the day. However, the lack of a marathon gave me a training itch that needed to be scratched, which is why I decided I would give the Nottingham Marathon a go instead. I'd never run around Nottingham before (unless you count being chased by a load of Forest fans back in the mid-eighties) so I had no idea what to expect when I lined up with several thousand others for the Robin Hood Marathon wearing a hat that bore the legend 'Run like an Animal.' Quite which animal I run like has been the source of some debate among my friends, with suggestions ranging from sloth and one-legged duck, to giraffe and retired greyhound.

The combination of great course and twattish hat combined to help me achieve a finishing time of 2:56:53, a PB at that time by 10 minutes and my first sub-3 hour marathon. As usual I had set off too fast because I never, ever learn and because the start was a mixed marathon/ half marathon start so I was pulled along by the pace of the half-marathoners, running the first mile in 6.23. 'Calm down,' I told myself. I ran the second mile in 6.40. 'Easy tiger,' I told myself. I ran the third mile in 6.45. 'You IDIOT,' I told myself. Anyway I was feeling good so I pushed on and managed to hold a 6.50 pace for miles 4,

5, 6 etc. The course cruelly took us within yards of the half marathon finish before peeling off for lap two, and I reached the halfway point in 1.26 thinking, 'Hmmmm – this is probably all going to go wrong soon.' The crowds thinned out dramatically for the second half of the run but I kept up the 6.50s and I was somewhat pleased to reach the 20 mile mark in 2.11, which was a PB for that distance and had me thinking 'Hmmmm – this is probably all going to go wrong soon.' By the point we reached the giant rowing lake at Holme Pierrepoint I was trying (and failing) to work out the maths in my head of whether I could beat 3 hours if the wheels didn't come off. This continued for miles 22, 23 and 24 and it wasn't until mile 25 that even I was able to work out that I had a bit of time in hand. This also coincided with the first signs of trouble as my time slowed to 7.19 for the mile.

With 200 yards to go not even a bunch of rampaging Forest fans would have stopped me and I crossed the line in a happy and somewhat surprised frame of mind. So far, so good and no sign of any of the trouble I've promised to tell you about. My distracted elation may account for what I did next, which may even yet see me end up on some sort of register. In the morning before the race I'd left my car in the designated parking area, which happened to be right next to a children's playground. On returning to my car I began the usual ritual of getting my sweaty kit off and getting my compression tights and dry clothes on. This was complicated by performing this feat inside the car so as to avoid public nudity, and also involved me picking congealed jelly babies from my shorts pocket and lobbing them out the window. In a moment of awful clarity it suddenly occurred to me that I was sitting in a car, naked from the waist down, throwing sweets out of my window at a children's play area … I quickly fought a pitched battle with my Skins to get them on my legs as fast as possible, which made the car rock violently from one side to the other, which made things look even worse. I then screeched out of the car park like a getaway driver, all the while muttering 'It's not what it looks like, officer' and wondering whether I should stop and rip the registration plates off the car in a bid to avoid having to stand before m'learned colleagues in Melton Mowbray again.

**Trouble number three**
Years ago, when my dad got sent to jail, he didn't take it well at all. He refused all offers of food and drink, spat and swore at anyone who came near him and smeared his 'business' all over the walls. That was the last time we ever played Monopoly. Joking aside, there has always been a competitive streak in the Brunts and despite my early sporting failures at school I've clearly inherited this gene, although the outlet for my competitiveness is, bizarrely, cross-country running, the running discipline at which I am least talented. For those of you unfamiliar with this pastime, it involves men and women congregating in a wet field, donning vests with the word 'Harriers' on the back and then running over a series of hills and bogs before crossing a finish line made of two canes and a bit of tape where an old bloke gives you a metal disc and a withering look. Some of the more sadistic courses include a stream to jump across where the vicious crowds gather

to watch some poor sod go headfirst into the murky bilge. I'm sure it's only a matter of time before you have to complete some kind of obstacle while under fire from a machine-gunner. The races are divided between a bunch of stick-thin burger-dodgers at the front who float over the ground and complete circuits faster than the Large Hadron Collider, and a bunch of carthorses at the back who plough through the ground like human tractors. Unsurprisingly I belong to the latter category but, like a growing number of triathletes, I've latched on to cross-country as a great way to build strength and to distract yourself from the soul-sucking darkness between January and March as well as all the sunny-side-up halfwits claiming spring is almost here.

I also enjoy the cut-throat competitiveness of these races, which seem to give more scope for team tactics and individual treachery than any of the other sports I do. Points are awarded to your club based on your finishing position but, although these are team events, it tends to be your clubmates that you try hardest to beat, and if you show any kind of comradeship you'll probably be handed a copy of *Das Kapital* and given 48 hours to leave the country. I frequently get into trouble at cross-country races because there's something about being barged out of the way that makes me see red. One year I did the Midland Masters (OAPs) Cross Country championships amid the wasteland scavengers of Wolverhampton and was toiling near the back only to be shoved out of the way by another runner as he cut inside me on a corner. I'm not exactly sure what happened next because everything went blurry and shouty, making the world look like an Al Qaeda video, and the next thing I knew I was sprinting over the line in fifteenth place, collecting a gold medal as part of the winning team. I virtually crippled myself in the process and left myself with a pulled Achilles, which still hurts to this day. Additionally, although I hammered the guy who shoved me, I had to endure all his post-race excuses for why he lost, using rich and vibrant language that enabled him to sound knowledgeable despite being what we linguists call 'a knob' – and thanks to my throbbing legs I couldn't get away!

**Trouble number four**
It is written in *The Triathletes' Bible* that: 'Thou shalt not enter running races unless thou cycleth to them, nor shalt thou do a swimming event unless thou runneth during the interval, and after any cycling time-trial thou shalt jump off thy bike and go for a hard run – otherwise thy races do not count and thou cannot braggeth on Facebook.' As a result of this unspoken code, I found myself planning to race in a swimming gala on the Isle of Wight followed swiftly by an entirely separate ten-mile run near Poole. No cycling sadly, although had there been a pedalo for hire at Cowes I'd have had a go at using it to reach Portsmouth. I had a good reason for wanting to migrate southwards because an upshot of my medal-winning run mentioned a moment ago was that, having seen what I'm capable of when not dossing about, my running club tried to rope me into doing the national championships in the buzzing metropolis of Sunderland. The prospect of eight hours of driving to run 12k in a mudpit – in the rain,

in Sunderland – sounded as much fun as listening to One Direction playing banjos. Instead, I skeddadled off to the Isle of Wight, which is as far away from Sunderland as it possible to be while remaining earth-bound.

I was joined in my island adventures by my mate Keith Burdett, previously introduced to you as a bleached Wookie but who, on reflection, looks more like Father Ted's stunt double. We travelled down and stayed over in my campervan, which is always a risk because spending time with your mates on holiday dramatically increases the risk of finding out what they are really like. Keith is a mild-mannered man until you add water, at which points he becomes an instant headcase who views all his competitors with the same hostility as a cornered badger, to the point where anyone attempting to swim in the same lane as him is likely to get their teeth knocked down their throat. It is also written in *The Triathletes' Bible* that: 'Thou shalt try to beat thy mates above all others' so, despite the presence of lots of other competitors, the fiercest rivalry was the Brunt vs Burdett celebrity death-match.

The first part of the DIY-Tri challenge involved doing seven swimming races in a day and first blood went to Keith who trounced me in the 800m freestyle. Revenge was mine in the 100m medley, and after that we set about thrashing each other until even our hair hurt. Honours ended reasonably even before we legged it for the last evening ferry crossing, which we made by the skin of Keith's dentures. It was thus late and cold when we arrived at our Dorset campsite on Saturday night, and the atmosphere was also frosty when I jokingly implied to the stuffy campsite owners that Keith and I were a couple, a comment that went down like a horse in a burger. Fortunately, I concealed the subsequent awkward silence by saying, 'Well, this is awkward,' and, even though I later explained that we were in the area because of swimming and running races, we spent the rest of our stay being studiously ignored by the campsite owners and all the stuck-up gits who would only know what a triathlete was if one ran their quirky local cheesemongers.

Part *deux* of the DIY-Tri was the ten-miler, a hilly run around country lanes near Poole that was also doubling as the National Masters ten-mile championship ('Masters' sounds so much nicer than 'decrepit old farts'). There were plenty of very handy runners there but, of course, the only race that mattered was Brunt vs Burdett as the world's most competitive middle-aged men lined up against each other. It ended in narrow victory for Brunt – otherwise I wouldn't have written about it – but Keith got some measure of revenge by farting in the campervan on the way home and almost rendering me unconscious. The trouble came when I was halfway back to Coventry and my mobile phone rang. It was one of the race organisers calling.

'Where are you?' he asked.

'Halfway home,' I said.

'Any chance you could come back, only you've won gold in the 40–45 age group and we want to present it to you.'

The reason I had left so promptly was that I was under strict orders to get back home in order to attend a Nuremberg Rally (visit to my mum's house) so I was now presented with a dilemma – turn back to accept the gold medal and crowd adulation that comes with being a national champion but condemn myself to a week of living in a house with the atmosphere of a tomb for being late agaaaaain, or carry on home and risk upsetting the organising body of a sport not noted for its warmth and flexibility of rule application. In the end I opted to head home, mostly because the fuel costs of heading back would have bankrupted me. I asked for the medal to be posted to me – which took *six months* to sort out, by which time no one I'd told believed I'd ever won a medal let alone become a national champion. And, as we all know, it doesn't count if no one believes you.

## Trouble number five

This is perhaps the biggest one of all because it involves someone uttering eight words to me that completely changed my life. It's ridiculous to think that eight simple words, spoken by someone you barely know, can lead to a total change in your world that affects who you are, what you are, what you look like, where you go, who your friends are, how much money you have and what you do with all your time. The year was 2003 and the place was back at good old Barclays Bank. It was the day after I had completed the London Marathon and I was walking into the office like my legs had been placed in callipers. Despite being in agony I was proudly holding aloft my finisher's medal and accepting the plaudits of my colleagues (who didn't realise how genuinely poor my performance had been) when a woman called Sally Plummridge said something that unleashed a catastrophic chain of events that would lead you – yes you – to be reading these somewhat overpriced words at this very moment. She said ... 'I bet you couldn't do the London Triathlon' ...

# Chapter 6

I imagine you've reached this point in the book wondering when I'm going to start talking about triathlons, given that's what this book is meant to be about. Well, I've always believed that if you're doing the dance of the seven veils, it's best to slowly remove the veils one at a time, not just rip them all off at once and whip your tackle out. So you'll be pleased (!) to know that it's tackle-out time now as we begin to talk all things tri. Although this book is all about my quest for Ironman greatness, it took me some years of farting about before I summed up the courage to do one. In fact, my first ever memory of Ironman came long before I took up any kind of athletics. I was watching the telly in the early-nineties when Ironman Hawaii was briefly covered on the news with those 'kerrrrazzy' athletes viewed with the same apparent respect as a novelty news item about a dog that could say 'sausages'. I remember being agog at the distances involved and thinking 'I'd never be able to do that.' Then the video for 'Summertime Love' by Sabrina came on and I forgot all about it.

My route to triathlon came via running with an episode we covered in the last chapter and which I won't repeat lest you feel short-changed enough to ask for a refund. It does strike me as ridiculous, though, how your whole life can basically turn round as the result of eight words – 'I bet you couldn't do the London Triathlon.' When the lovely Sally uttered those words I didn't even know what a triathlon was, but from the dim recollection I have, I signed up for the race online on the spot. There were two to choose from, a sprint distance (750 metre swim, 20 kilometre cycle, 5 kilometre run) or an Olympic distance (1500 metre swim, 40 kilometre cycle, 10 kilometre run), and I think you now know me well enough to make an educated guess which one of those I entered. Drawbacks to entering the race included the facts that:

1.  I didn't own a wetsuit, had no idea how to get one, and had never swum in anything but a swimming pool in my life. The swim leg of this race would take place in London's Royal Victoria Dock where, as well as other swimmers, I would face an array of floating turds and perhaps the occasional body of a gangland hit victim.

2.  I didn't own a bike and had not ridden one since I left school, when I abandoned cycling in order to borrow my mum's car and impress girls as much as one can while leaning out of the window of a brown Datsun Cherry. A bloke I knew at work called Tom was an occasional weekend cyclist who owned a road bike, which I asked to borrow and which he refused to lend, something I stored in my grudge bank for years. Then I bumped into him while out cycle training, whereupon I rode with him and put him through the pain-wringer so badly that he stopped, got off his bike and sagged into a ditch with a face that looked like he'd been ducking for apples in a chip pan.

3.  As we have seen I was, at this time, extremely poor at running.

Never mind, though. I wasn't about to let any of this stand in the way of a bet and nipped any negative thoughts in the knackers by hiring a bike and a wetsuit from a shop, digging out the same crappy trainers I'd done the London Marathon in, and training myself to become a triathlete. At first this largely involved replacing my usual breakfast of a thrice fried bap with muesli and bananas, and shaving off the long hairs on my legs that made my knees look like an elderly Rastafarian. I can still see Nicky's bewildered look as she tried to work out why the bathwater was taking so long to drain away.

My career as a cyclist started inauspiciously when my new bike was delivered to my parents' house and I grew concerned that Dad had gone off to the pub on it. As unlikely as this sounds, he had form for this sort of thing. I once had a box of twelve bottles of wine delivered to his house for me, and when I opened it at home it only contained eleven, which my dad claimed was an alarming rate of evaporation that showed global warming is a dangerous reality. When I eventually unpacked my new bike and rode up the lane, I genuinely didn't have the faintest idea how the gears worked, and was trying hard to master the toe clips – yes toe clips – without ending up in a hedge.

Cornering was a particular challenge for me and I appeared to have the turning circle of a hippo with a javelin through its head. I set about remedying this by riding round and round my patio in a very small circle, which looked like I was training to race on the world's smallest velodrome, much to the amusement of my neighbours. The bike was called a CLX, which sounded like a brand of piles ointment. I set about doing training rides of 25 miles around the lanes where I live – never more than 25 miles, never on any other roads and never with any variety of pace because doing 25 miles was challenge enough judging by the fact that the first time I tried it I fell asleep in the shower afterwards. I then spent an hour applying chafe cream to my legs, which looked like they'd been set on fire and then put out with a golf shoe. Having sort of learned my lesson from the London Marathon, I also did some actual running outside on roads, and even went to my local pool with my wetsuit on to try and get used to the sensation of swimming with something so tight across my groin that I could have passed for a Bee Gee.

It was around this time that, in a bid to acquire super-powers without extra effort, I started taking vitamin tablets. I'd read somewhere about a cyclist called Lance Armstrong who said he needed to take supplements (and by God did he!) so I started chuffing Sanatogen like it was going out of fashion. One side effect I didn't know about when I started popping pills was that certain vitamins turn your wee fluorescent yellow, and it was just my luck that the moment of discovery came at half-time of a football match I'd gone to watch. Having jostled my way to the front of the crowded urinal I proceeded to let fly with a glow-in-the-dark jet of water, which came as a surprise not only to me but also to my near neighbours as my Day-Glo pee lazily made its way along the bottom of the communal trough. One by one heads turned to stare at me and I was aware of people steadily inching away. I felt I owed some sort of explanation but saying, 'I take vitamins' in this kind of company would be tantamount to saying, 'I press wild flowers and like Kylie Minogue' – a swift pummelling would follow, so instead I said, 'Stay off the lemon vodka,' and nearly ruptured my diaphragm trying to get it over with before legging it out of the bogs.

Looking back now with the benefit of ten years of triathlon incompetence, er, insight behind me, it is staggering to think that I thought this was going to end in anything but disaster, but as we have learned I have never been one to take much notice of, well, anything really. At that time having a training plan reeked to me of being the equivalent of having life goals, and nothing said, 'You're a loser' more than having a personal motivational phrase about being a winner. Such was my all-encompassing ignorance of triathlon that ten minutes before the race I decided it would be a good idea to buy a bottle cage and a drinks bottle to put on my bike because it was feeling a bit warm – 32° Celsius warm to be precise.

Chucking myself into Royal Victoria Dock didn't faze me in the slightest, although I have subsequently learned that this is the part of the race most newbies dread, and with memories of my former swimming abilities fresh in my mind I plonked myself at the front of the wave. I suspected I may be slightly out of my league a few minutes into the swim when, as I was in full front crawl flight, I was overtaken by a bloke doing breaststroke. I was, in fact, one of the very last to leave the water and lurch up the dockside gangplank like I had a wooden leg. The transition was inside the Excel Centre, which has all the architectural charm of a loading bay and I was off on the old pile-cream-machine towards the attractive flyovers of Bermondsey. The bike course was a two-lap affair and I remember starting to feel distinctly hot and tired during the second lap, which seemed remarkably free of other cyclists thanks to the pace I was maintaining. I arrived back to a transition area full of bikes and headed out into the now blistering sunshine for a three-lap run.

To my credit, I managed to run the first lap at a pace that would do credit to the swiftest steamroller ever built as I battled to keep my cadence up and my breakfast down. Laps two and three were conducted at a more leisurely pace (I walked) before I found enough dignity to run the final half-a-kilometre over the finish line where I had to be held upright by a skinny old marshal, making it look like I was being carted off by the grim reaper. My finishing time was a whopping 3 hours 20 minutes although the finish line photos suggest I was well pleased with my efforts. This may possibly be because I am the only person ever to pass through Bermondsey wearing a pair of Lycra shorts and live to tell the tale, but more likely because I never dreamed I would do anything like this ever gain.

Further evidence of the fact that I have become an Ironman by accident comes from what happened next. Despite a time so slow that I had to buy a mobile phone with a longer screen so I didn't have to scroll down so far on the results page to see my finishing position, I had sort of enjoyed myself and was consequently feeling more conflicted than Anakin Skywalker about whether to do anything like this ever again. A week or so later I was over in Birmingham shopping and, to kill some time while Nicky was in Next looking at some bloody thing or other, I bought a copy of *220 Triathlon* magazine, the one I would end up writing for. I was standing outside Next leafing through it and staring with wonder at the shiny carbon items contained within when I became aware of a couple staring at me. After checking my flies to make sure that wasn't the reason, I smiled weakly whereupon they asked, 'Are you a triathlete?' It turns out that both of them were triathletes. The chap's name was Paul Kingscott, one of the stalwarts of the Black Country Tri club. It hadn't occurred to me that there were clubs that did this sort of thing, but Paul informed me that there was even one on my doorstep known as Coventry Triathletes.

Clearly, it was meant to be that I should become a triathlete, what with the chain of coincidences at work and even out shopping, which conspired to pitch me headlong into the sport. I'm not one to fight fate, so I decided I'd get in touch with the Coventry club and find out more. The first person I spoke to was none other than Mark Stewart, now my fellow would-be Roth-man, er Challenger etc, who invited me to the club's weekly swimming session. A week later I duly turned up to meet Mark. The second person I met was Steve Howes, the Iceman from our channel swim and someone of whom you will hear more later in this book. I remember being massively intimidated by the race T-shirts everyone was wearing – such intimidation being an important skill in the triathlon world – and feeling distinctly out of place as a Zeppelin-sized laughing stock who couldn't have looked less fit if I'd been smoking 40 fags a day through an asbestos cigarette holder. I'd always assumed cyclists were the kind of weirdy-beardies who owned Dido CDs and recycled jumper fluff but here was a bunch of very sinewy men and women who couldn't have swum faster if they'd been fired out of a U-boat, particularly a man called Mike McGillion who said he was an expert in inflation, which turned out to mean he sold party balloons.

It was inevitable that, upon mixing with this company, I would be lured down the slippery slope from doing a triathlon to being a triathlete and within nine months of joining them I had done not one but TWO Half Ironmans. I'd also returned to the London Triathlon and taken an hour off my previous finishing time. Not only that, but the gut that pressed against my belt like a balloon full of mud had vanished to be replaced with the muscle-bound Adonis you see before you to this day, if you have conjunctivitis. No longer did I look like a flabby-faced toff about to steal the chips off your plate when your back was turned. The catalyst for this transformation was simply that I had found a group of people I liked, who were willing to allow some hapless cock-end to train with them, and who opened up the arcane world of triathlons to me, showing me where the races were, and how to enter in that nanosecond between online race entries opening and the red banner arriving that says 'Race Full'.

These days I am so experienced that I am handing out words of wisdom to newbies myself, constantly stunned at how my elevation to a kind of triathlon-idiot-savant could possibly have happened. This was apparent recently at a race put on by my club – still Coventry Triathletes – when I was asked to give a talk to people who were doing the race for the first time, advising them about what to expect. One glance at my shambling semi-existence should have revealed to them that I can't even be trusted to give advice about how to sit the right way round on a toilet, but this didn't stop people listening rapt with attentiveness as I bullshitted massively about what I had achieved in the sport. Watching the newbies race while I was marshalling out on the bike course of that race was also instructive for me because I learned that I am not alone when it comes to some of the weirder habits I have picked up from doing triathlons.

For example, sometimes I talk to the weather. I realise this makes me sound as sane as the secret lovechild of Josef Fritzl and Glenn Hoddle, but while cycling I regularly shout at the wind, which stays in my face whichever way I turn, bellowing 'Is that all you've got!', or stare up at the rainclouds saying, 'You just couldn't hold off for half a fucking hour could you?' I'm barely suppressing an all-encompassing rage equal to football's greatest nark merchants. I'd always assumed this was just my steady descent into bumbling senility but no, it seems I am not alone and that other triathletes are weather-talkers, too. In fact, m'lud, I put it to you that triathletes not only talk to the elements but they also talk to their bikes, to cars, to potholes, to junctions, to their legs and to themselves.

My particular job on my club's race day was to stand on a traffic island in a rectangular yellow bib that made me look like SpongeBob SquarePants, pointing at approaching cyclists and shouting, 'TURN LEFT!' This gave me an excellent vantage point to secretly sneer at people's cornering skills and to clearly hear what they were muttering to themselves as they rode past. I should point out that the weather was about as pleasant as being kicked in the shin by David Nalbandian, and the poor novices racing had to negotiate puddles you could breast-stroke in and rain so heavy I was contemplating building an ark. As a result, people had plenty to moan about and I was delighted to hear people chuntering away to themselves. The most popular mutters appeared to be 'Come on legs' when people stood up on the pedals to ride away from the roundabout, 'Piss off rain' as they approached the roundabout, and 'Oh, for fuck's sake!' when they had to stop for a car coming round the roundabout. Any clunking of gears was immediately reacted to by the rider looking down at their bike and saying, 'Get in, you bastard' while any cars that were slowly driving just ahead of the riders were treated to a strange Buddhist-like incantation that grew slowly in volume and went, 'Go-on-go-on-go-ON-GO-ON!!'

As an aside, this was my first experience of being a race marshal, and it mostly involved sitting around doing nothing – and in my case the devil makes work for idle hands. Some of my mates were racing, so I thought I would lift their spirits by holding up a large card with a certain four-letter word that rhymes with my surname scrawled on it as they rode by. I'm pleased to say that it did the trick and not only distracted them from the rain, it almost caused them to crash. As well as abusing triathletes, my duties also involved justifying my presence to passing motorists and explaining the legalities of racing on roads to outraged hypocrites and the exceptionally slow-witted. Mostly, I had drivers shaking their head at me if they were delayed by a nanosecond by a rider at the roundabout, and handily I had my hand-drawn sign to hold up to them. One lady wound down her window to demand, 'Who gave you permission for this!', to which I replied, 'The Lord Jesus Christ,' which is always an answer that gets you left alone. Although many racers were busy chatting to themselves, quite a few did shout a 'thanks marshal' as they went by, and that was genuinely lovely because sitting on a roundabout in the pouring rain, watching melanin-deprived triathletes wearing expressions that made them look like a face trapped in a haunted mirror, is slightly less pleasant than a piss-bomb exploding in a skip full of rusty forks. If ever asked to marshal again I will claim that the date clashes with the opportunity to go to Twycross Zoo, coat my clinkers in honey and dangle them over the bear enclosure.

After competing in triathlons for a few years the whole thing can occasionally seem somewhat routine and a typical Olympic distance race for me these days goes roughly thus:

4.00 a.m. – My alarm goes off. My instant thought is 'sod the race' and I go back to sleep until I remember I've paid a £60 entry fee. I doze until five past, then 10 past, then quarter past – what is it about getting up that means you will only do it when the time ends in a five or a zero?

4.15 a.m. – A double espresso in the morning really jolts you awake – especially if you have it as an enema.

4.20 a.m. – I spend ten minutes deciding which T-shirt to wear so I can show off while I'm racking my bike. Do I wear an Ironman shirt or, because it's an Olympic distance race, should I wear a GB team shirt – or would wearing an international shirt to a local race make people think I'm a knob? I opt for a 2004 Olympic finisher's T-shirt to imply I'm experienced, but which just means that I probably have fillings older than most of the other competitors.

4.30 a.m. – I stare at the kit I've unpacked from my bag because of the nagging feeling I've forgotten something due to the lack of sleep making my brain so dense that light actually bends round it. I physically enact the process of putting kit on in T1 and T2 while muttering a strange incantation that goes 'sock, sock, shoe, shoe, race belt, sunglasses, helmet, gel, GO' so it looks like I'm doing some kind of weird t'ai chi exercise.

4.31 a.m. – I make up my energy drinks. How many scoops of powder is it per bottle? I can't remember. God, I'm useless, I hate me, I think I'll put ten scoops in, which should at least take the edge off my failure.

6.00 a.m. – I'm in transition laying out my kit, and watching as people stumble around trying to balance their kit boxes on top of their tri bars. One of my favourite parts of any triathlon is the walk into transition before a race, where I amuse myself watching people trying to balance a plastic box containing their kit on top of their bike. I'm not sure who first decided that carting all your kit around in a box was de rigueur for triathletes, but balancing a foot-square rigid cube on top of an inch-wide circular tube, while it's moving, is a catastrophically inefficient means of transportation. I take perverse pleasure in watching people's tempers flare as their bikes slide away from beneath their grip, cracking them meatily on the shin, or hearing the lavish swearing as the box tips over scattering their kit like a cluster bomb. These days I avoid this humiliation by keeping my kit in a contraption known as a 'bag', which can be slung over one's shoulder and which also enables me to ride my bike right up to the transition entrance rather than walk, making me look experienced, manly and slightly sexy. Being experienced has its downsides though because I'm surrounded by people who are twenty years younger than me. So in my 2004 finisher's T-shirt I feel as self-conscious as a chimp with a viola. A man wearing a GB skinsuit walks past and the lad next to me mutters 'knob.'

6.55 a.m. – Wetsuit on.

6.55 a.m. and 10 seconds – I realise I've also forgotten the stuff to rub on my neck to prevent chafing. I KNEW there was something.

7.00 a.m. – The race starts.

7.00 a.m. and 10 seconds – My wetsuit starts rubbing my neck.

7.22 a.m. – I exit the water. Someone has been tapping my toes for the past five minutes; however I have been weeing down the legs of my wetsuit, so we're even. I run in to transition and try to look like I'm not checking out how many bikes are still there.

8.00 a.m. – I'm out on the bike course. I eat an energy bar, which basically tastes like textured air. I overtake some people and some people overtake me, so I make a note of their kit so I can get them back on the run, and I kid myself this is realistic. I pass a man who's had a puncture. 'That's one place higher up the leader board,' I think to myself. Overall, my sympathy could fit into a Japanese thimble.

8.30 a.m. – I'm in T2 going through the 'shoe, shoe, sunglasses etc' thing for real, although the 'shoe, shoe' bit is harder when every leg bend threatens to give you cramp.

8.45 a.m. – I've done one lap of the run course. I overtake some kits I recognise from the bike course, and a man in a GB skinsuit about whom I mutter 'knob.'

9.15 a.m. – I will finish in about 2 hours 15 minutes and some seconds. I next scan the results to work out that

I have finished in the top ten (yes, that means ninth), and, realising that I haven't, I look to see if I have finished in the top ten in my age group. Realising that I haven't, I try to refine this some more until I work out that I'm in the top three of men over 40 from the West Midlands, which is what I'll tell my friends. I put on my finisher's T-shirt, and so begins its 12-month journey from flavour-of-the-month, to running top, to bottom of the drawer to bike-cleaning rag.

10.15 a.m. – I stop at the services on the drive home because I'm starving. The sandwiches all look disgusting and exactly what people who are too lazy to put their own stuff between bread deserve, so I opt for a bag of breadcrumbed abattoir scrapings. The services are full of people who are all staring at me, possibly because my breath smells like I've slept with a tramp's toe in my mouth, possibly because I'm walking like I've been kicked very hard in the coccyx, but most likely because I'm wearing a skinsuit unzipped to the waist, compression socks and a T-shirt that says something like 'Big Cow Racing' on the front.

11.00 a.m. – I'm home. I haven't won the race, but I haven't finished near the back either. I saw some friends, I got some new tan-lines and I've lost another sock. The world hasn't changed, women are not now looking at me in a different, more sultry manner and I have not acquired a group of slim, toned friends with witty facial hair who sit around in light airy rooms laughing as they Bluetooth each other.

It has taken me years of turning up and farting out deeply average results to achieve this kind of efficiency, but in rare moments of self-awareness I still sometimes wonder what my life would be like if Sally Plummridge hadn't said those eight words, or if I hadn't bought a *220 Triathlon* magazine, or if Paul Kingscott hadn't been walking past and spoken to me and made me think, 'Hmm, these triathletes seem like a friendly bunch.' Not that I am now the perfect triathlon machine, by the way, as my current training for Challenge Roth continues to reveal. Even ten years on from my first Olympic-distance race I don't get them completely right and I continue to have more weaknesses than the Maginot Line. Let's be honest, every superhero has their Achilles heel. Superman has kryptonite, Achilles had his, er, heel, and Lindsay Lohan had several Ketel One vodkas. I am no different, only my Achilles heel is a bit more abundant than kryptonite – it's rain.

I realise that this book may contain the odd factual error because of clones, evil counterparts from other dimensions, shape-shifting demons and the illusions of villainous magicians. Trust me, however, when I say that I despise racing in the rain as much as Jeremy Kyle presumably despises himself. The reason for this loathing is, of course, fear. As a result of several wet-race bike crashes over the years I now regard every rainy road as being covered in ice-encrusted glass and thus the most dangerous strip of tarmac outside of a *Mad Max* film. Never was this more evident than in my first race of this season, which was an Olympic-distance race in the Midlands. I entered it as an early leg-stretcher for what awaits me in Roth. I realised I might be in for a trying day when I woke at 6.00 a.m. to the sound of hail drumming on my campervan roof. I attempted to make breakfast but got tired of a pre-race meal consisting mainly of rainwater, so gave up and went to a local café to join the truckers for their early-morning fry up. It's always a joy to share a table with a man who has sinus issues, a T-shirt with a *Star Wars* joke on it and an astounding conception of what constitutes personal hygiene.

By the time it came to drive to the race and start racking my bike in transition and faffing about with my kit, the weather had mercifully dried up but the presence of black clouds overhead was making me more edgy than a broken pisspot. The last thing I needed was a chatty transition neighbour with views about the weather – so right on cue my neighbour cast his gaze skywards and said, 'Looks like rain,' which made me want to belt him so hard across the shins with a track pump that he started dry-heaving. In the event I said, 'Go away before I climb over this rack and slay you.' He seemed surprised but continued to talk about puddles on the course, which provoked my response, 'Go and arrange for someone to bury you cheaply, and I'll pay half the expense.' Oh, how I yearn for the good old days when you could tell people what you thought about them with a hatchet or a bow and arrows.

My race started promisingly with a new personal best of 21.20 for the 1500m swim – good news you might think, but it only served to accentuate what followed. The roads were still dry so I scampered along the first six miles of the course like a drugged up Power Ranger until we reached a sign that said 'Welcome to Wales.' I'm aware that until the seventies Wales was an undersea kingdom and it is making a concerted effort to return to its naturally submerged state, so sure enough, no sooner had we passed the 'Croeso' sign than the heavens opened. It didn't just rain, it chucked it down, and my fear and loathing instantly kicked in until I became about as comfortable on my bike as an early Christian martyr tied against a stake. My speed dropped to the point where I was worried about being overtaken by the fucking Karaoke Runner again and, to add an extra kick in the teeth, half the field overtook me.

This miserable experience lasted until we reached the 'Welcome to England' sign two miles from the end, whereupon it instantly dried up and I immediately turned into Chris Hoy and blasted into T2 like a curry-powered fart. My overall bike time was a weaselly 1:12.30, a full ten minutes slower than I normally do for this distance, with the added humiliation of being exposed as a cringing weakling. Stung by my cowardice and nicely rested after my gentle ride, I tore round the run as fast as anyone can when they basically look like an unbaked gingerbread man. My run time on a lumpy 10k was 37.30 despite running so hard that I had to hold my mouth shut to prevent myself from throwing up a warm glop of energy gels down my front.

So my training for Roth had started the way these things always start, with me questioning how in the name of our Lord Brownlee I was ever going to manage to cover 140.6 miles when I had just made such a hash of covering 30. And how the hell am I going to manage if it rains? Oh, and thank you Sally Plummridge, wherever you are, for starting all this by setting off a chain reaction that those scientists at Cern who are trying to make a black hole would be proud of. And I believe we said that the wager for me completing the London Triathlon was a tenner, which I have still not received even after a decade of waiting. Bloody bankers.

# Chapter 7

It is a piece of received triathlon wisdom that doing a few races as part of your build-up to an Ironman is a good idea, which is how I came to be racing in the rain in the Welsh-border badlands. Partly this is so you can get a sense of your form before your main event of the year, partly because they are good training sessions under race conditions, and partly because after a winter of knocking about with swimmers, cross country runners and other forms of aquatic life, you need to remind yourself how to do a triathlon at all. More specifically you need to re-learn how to perform a transition between swimming and cycling, and then cycling and running, without scampering around the transition area looking for your bike amid the many hundreds of identical overpriced carbon shapes. Many is the time I have seen early-season triathletes looking vainly for their bike, helmet, shoes, trainers, gels and competence before trying desperately to find the way out of transition amid the maze of bike racks and kitbags. I remember seeing one guy running three times round a particularly complicated transition in Belgium looking for the run exit shouting, 'Ariadne, the thread, the thread!' Being grammar-school educated meant I got this joke but from the po-faced reaction it got from others I guess that triathlon is not awash with classical scholars.

Finding the right balance between training to achieve peak fitness at just the right time (i.e. 6.59 a.m. on the morning of Challenge Roth), and knackering yourself out by doing too many warm-up races, is a fine balance to get right and one which my coach, Dave, plans to perfection for me, if only I did as he said. This year Dave and I decided I would do two Half Ironman races as a warm up, as well as a week of overseas cycling on training camp in Lanzarote to ensure I took to the start line with some top quality tan lines halfway up my arms and legs, the cultivation of several cycling and running tan lines of different lengths until you look like a walking barcode being an important way of marking you out as a triathlete. My plan to do just the two races didn't take account of two unforeseen factors though:

1. A brand new race had been organised right on my doorstep, organised by a friend of mine.

2. My friends were planning to do different races to me, and I am pathologically incapable of saying no when they suggest I should come and do their races with them.

So it was that on top of my planned races of the 'Kernowman' Half Ironman in  Cornwall and the Cotswold 113 Half Ironman in the, er, Cotswolds, I now added two further races, namely the excitingly titled 'Swashbuckler' and 'Avenger' – both of which were also Half Ironmans. This made a total of four middle distance races in my pre-Iron/Challenge/packet-of-fags build-up, exactly double the number that I needed. Ho hum as they say, and yet more evidence of the accidental nature of my approach to Ironmans. I like Half Ironmans, though, because with a 1900-metre swim, 56-mile cycle and 13-mile run they are usually over and done with inside a morning, you can usually fart them out without the training taking over your life for months on end, and they still have the word 'Ironman' in the title to make you sound impressive to the wider public who know no better. It's my favourite distance, so I've genuinely lost count of how many I have done over the years and I have travelled to such exotic locations as Monaco, Belgium, Weymouth, Milton Keynes and the dark side of the moon (Leicestershire) to do them, although this does not mean I have become wise in their ways.

For example, back in 2007 I was about to start a Half Ironman in the USA when I stubbed my foot on a rock and took the skin off the end of my big toe. This mishap was soon forgotten as I addressed the more pressing problem of trying to stop 2000 swimmers from booting my goggles off as we sprinted for the first buoy, or boooeeeey as Americans inexplicably call them. In fact, all thoughts of my skinless toe vanished until halfway round the bike course when I needed the loo and decided to save time by peeing while cycling. I hoiked up my shorts and began the freewheel of shame as I did the disgusting deed, at which point I was sharply reminded of my earlier foot-stubbery as some wee leaked into my shoe and hit my toe with the ferocity of a snapping turtle. As the stinging hit warp-factor 10 on my personal pain threshold, a shocked group of spectators were treated to the sight of a man streaking past them with his knob out and the haggard look of someone who fought at the Battle of Stalingrad.

I do not tell this story in support of personal hygiene, but to underline the point that this is how I learn my lessons – by making catastrophic mistakes. This makes me a dangerous person to seek advice from, as some novices tried to do at a Half Ironman last year when I was exposed as the most experienced triathlete at the race briefing. The race in question was the Ely Monsterman, a middle-distance dash around the flatlands of Cambridgeshire and in the pre-race pep talk people were asked to hold up their hands to indicate how many Half Ironmans they had done. When he reached six races, I was the only person in the room with arm still aloft and there were audible gasps when we worked out I'd done some unspecified number of middle distance races above 20. As soon as the briefing was over I was pounced on by first-timers asking questions; they seemed to revere me as some sort of triathlon Terminator with origins as a nude man who materialised in a transition area and whose first words were, 'I need your Oakleys, your Carnacs and your Cervelo P3.'

I had to repeatedly point out to them that despite being a triathlete for ten years I am basically triathlon's equivalent of Alan Shearer, in that we both spend much of our time commenting on a sport we clearly have no recollection of having participated in. I felt this was terribly important to stress to people trying to harness the terrifying power of my black hole of anti-knowledge. Fortunately the Ely Monstermunchers soon realised that I was not some sort of glowing, hovering brain with massive JCVD-style biceps when I started giving advice about how to unpeel your gel-covered hands from your handlebars as my top tip.

In truth, I've always recognised myself as a resolutely middle-of-the-pack athlete, a sort of triathlon equivalent of the house wine at a suburban Indian restaurant, and this image did not change in the first warm-up of my pre-Roth build up, the aforementioned 'Kernowman', which involved a jaunt around southern Cornwall with a sea-swim in the shadow of St Michael's Mount, a bike-leg down to Land's End and along the north Cornish coast, and a run on the slopes of Mount Everest, renamed on this occasion as Tregurtha Downs. I chose this particular race because Nicky is Cornish and she fancied a trip back to her homeland to stock up on proper pasties, saffron buns, clotted cream and a wicker man to burn her enemies in.

Despite a long journey down to the land of the Ewoks in my campervan, having one was well worth it when I arrived at the race venue because I was able to drive right up to the transition area in Marazion field, pull on the handbrake, unfurl my bed, stick the kettle on and scratch myself lavishly before going sleepy-bye-byes – and it's always pleasurable sitting on a chair as the sun sets watching some other poor schmuck having a duel to the death with a tent in the dark. The only downside to my van is that it has no loo and, thanks to my sneaky wee out of the door on the morning of the race, there is now a part of Marazion field that looks like it's been subjected to a scorched-earth attack where nothing will ever grow again, not even on a cellular level. The transition was a fairly as-you-please affair with a couple of bike racks set up in the field with some netting to make sure the accursed public were kept at bay, and the morning began with all the racers strolling together down to the beach to start the race. I can honestly say I love the more laid-back atmosphere of these kind of locally organised races compared with the high-intensity, nerve-shredding fandango you get before most Ironmans, which feel like you're in *The Shawshank Redemption* (only with more tunnelling through shit and no redemption.)

The race itself started inauspiciously for me because the sea was at the chillier end of hypothermic, which I found out when I plunged under the waves only to hurtle straight back up again cursing and spluttering like a sweary surface-to-air missile. Before the race we'd been told the water temperature was 11 degrees, and I think there might have been a decimal point missing from that number. Not being able to feel my limbs made for a slower-than-usual swim, although this did at least delay the effects of having not adjusted my wetsuit properly before diving in, and trapping a certain part of my private anatomy. Within minutes I was scanning the horizon for a railway line to lie across in a desperate attempt to remove the lower half of my body and relieve myself of the phenomenal pain being inflicted upon me. Although as a man I lack the required experience, I'm going to estimate that this was at least eleven times more painful than childbirth, and on exiting the water some lucky spectators were treated to the sight of me charging wildly into transition bellowing like a mountain gorilla with its toe caught in a mousetrap, and then cannonballing arse first on to the grass while tearing at the crotch of my wetsuit. The net effect of this experience turned my private parts into a maroon coloured bag of agony. I could now pass urine in three positions: standing, sitting and curled in a ball weeping.

The 56-mile bike leg was much less eventful apart from one motorist, who I'd describe as an enthusiastic self-partner, sitting two inches behind my rear wheel through the town of Hayle. I always say there's no better way for a driver to signal that he wants to go faster than by increasing the chance of my death by 40 per cent. Happily 99 per cent of the course was on scenic lanes along the Cornish coast with no traffic, which was excellent because race-day motorists are usually about as endearing as a gang of Nazi wasps. A quick stop for a wee up the side of a barn was witnessed by a passing local who suggested that I'd missed a bit of my shoulders when applying sun cream and that I was looking 'as burnt as a crow.' I worked very hard on the bike to make up for my swim, so by the time I set off on the half-marathon I was starting to look like the lone equine survivor of a fire at a donkey sanctuary.

The run course was extremely hilly with long off-road sections. Fortunately, inspiration was on hand because Nicky's parents, who have a summer caravan in nearby Porthtowan, had come down to cheer me on enthusiastically, although I noted this enthusiasm didn't extend to her dad putting his teeth in. All his toothless encouragement to 'Picksssshhh your knesssshh up' had the desired effect, though, and I was soon shuffling along. After just 90 minutes I was skipping over the line for my highest ever finishing position, with a pint of Skinners in one hand and a pasty in the other. In terms of being a good warm-up for Roth it couldn't have gone any better. If nothing else, it proved I've got the drive, the desire and the tenacity to be whatever I want to be, and the only thing holding me back is myself – and the two-year suspended prison sentence for what I did during that last lager blackout.

My next move after becoming a Kernowman was to attend a coaching talk given by Malcolm Brown MBE, former running coach for UK Athletics and current coach to the Brownlees, Non Stanford and various other professional triathletes who seem to have been getting the hang of the sport. I was hoping to absorb some wisdom from the man who has coached athletes to World and Olympic level because I'm fed up of looking for athletic advice on the internet, which appears to be plastered with adverts for baldness clinics, poor quality university courses, and gadgets that will solve all my training needs in exchange for a giant number made of coins and money. I'm sure marketing types think all triathletes sleep in a giant rustling money nest with a life-mantra of 'If you can't beat them, buy something.' Malcolm's talk was fascinating and what I actually learned was that the Brownlees are in fact robots, that what appears to be sweat on their brows is in fact a metallic sheen, and that when they get tired they are merely plugged into a USB port by which they are recharged. By now you've probably got the suspicion that this might be utter cock, and you'd be right, but the truthful point was that the Brownlees have led active lifestyles since they were toddlers (frankly they're still bloody toddlers when you're pushing 45), so when it came to taking up triathlons they had a fantastic base fitness on which to build. This was enormously useful news to me because as we have discussed already, as a kid in the seventies the only exercise we got was avoiding the groping hands of Radio 1 DJs. Thus the complete absence of an active lifestyle for the first 35 years of my life gave me a handy excuse for why I haven't won Kona – or indeed anything – yet, and helped keep any pressure of expectation off my shoulders during my preparations for Roth.

An equally educational experience came when, a fortnight later, it was time for me to do the Swashbuckler Middle Distance Tri which I had been talked into by my friend Joe (he of the five daughters and no hair) who was also training for Roth and who was bored since the police came and took his bong away. The race took place in the New Forest at an idyllic spot called Bucklers Hard with a swim in the harbour, a cycle around the scenic lanes between Beaulieu and Brockenhurst (giving way to ponies at all times), and a run around some lanes which may be equally scenic but which I didn't notice because I banged my nut on the bike rack in transition so spent most of the run clutching my head like I'd been clobbered by the riot police.

Again it was campervan time. I also drove Joe down with me with both our bikes perched precariously on the back. Normally, sleeping arrangements in the van involve me in the downstairs compartment on a pull-out, upholstered, comfy bed surrounded by noise-deadening metal walls and amenities such as sink, stove, spotlights, radio and pornography. My guests are usually condemned to the upstairs compartment aka the pop-top roof which involves a wafer-thin mattress, canvas walls and several midges who seem to live up there. However, Joe had no plans to be my live-in lodger and had brought his own tent to sleep in, on account of having a bladder the size of a squash ball that forces him to get up three times a night. At our pre-race campsite I slept the sleep of the righteous, cocooned in my tin box on wheels, listening to the muffled bickering of Joe giving the length of his tongue (6 and three-quarter inches) to some dickhead who was using a noisy generator to power the reading light in his tent.

With the race starting at 6.00 a.m. the next day, bike racking was conducted in a largely semi-conscious state and again I enjoyed the relaxed 'as-you-please' nature of the arrangements. The transition was on a first-come-first-served basis with people setting up their bikes in the most tactically advantageous spot for themselves – in my case this was next to the bike exit, and in Joe's case next to the Portaloos. The grass on the barefoot walk to the swim start was freezing so I prepared for the race by stamping on the ground like I was blasting away at the earth's crust in search of shale gas, while a weary Joe contented himself with doing massive yawns, which, without his teeth in, was like peering over the rim of a damp bucket. The swim was in the natural harbour and timed to take advantage of the highest tide and fewest number of gin-palaces heave-hoeing out of the anchorage. Having selected my starting position as usual to keep the maximum number of swimmers on my right and the maximum number of teeth in my head I awaited the klaxon in a relaxed frame of mind, practising for the Roth start by winding Joe up about how punchy the swim was going to be. The swim came and went in its usual maelstrom of thrashing about. I was swimming alongside someone whose pace and stroke count matched mine exactly, the only difference between us being that he kept trying to swim me into the sodding boats and I kept trying to send him out to sea. I emerged from the water in a little over 30 minutes, unleashed a massive salty burp on the spectators gathered on the slipway and set about getting out on the bike.

When I started out doing triathlons, aero helmets were a rare sight but nowadays they are so common that if you aren't wearing one you might as well have a saucepan on your head, so I felt a little self-conscious that I wasn't wearing mine on account of the weather forecast for the day being hot-hot-hot. Despite my lack of head-related aerodynamism I rode hard, taking advantage of a largely flat, extremely beautiful and slightly short course to clock up another fast-ish bike time – look out Roth, here I come! The run, however, was another matter and after a bright start involving passing lots of clearly inferior athletes, I progressively slowed throughout the 14-mile course and was passed by lots of clearly superior athletes who were better at pacing themselves. After a final lurch up the hill to the finish, I crossed the line with the words 'Fetch me a bucket quick!'

Still, I was happy enough with my performance, especially as this was the first time I'd done the Swashbuckler and rarely had I enjoyed a race more. Not only did I again race well but I also showed that doing two Half Ironmans in the space of three weeks was no barrier to future Roth-dominance, PLUS I got a top quality pirate-shaped finisher's medal at the end (and that's a proper shiver-me-timbers pirate rather than the Somali version). It was at the finish where I had an educational experience that put my plans for race domination at Roth into some perspective. Having finished in 4:53.07 for fiftieth-ish place, I was sauntering back to my bike in transition when I got chatting to one of the athletes from the Thames Turbo club who had used the race as their club championship.

'How did you get on?' he asked.

'4.53,' I replied, with a note of pride. 'How about yourself?'

'Eighth,' he answered, with genuine nonchalance before moving the conversation on to plans for the season ahead. Reality 1, Ego 0. Soon after this, I bumped into Ed Kirk-Wilson, the considerably more talented brother of my posh friend Will, a man who runs in the style of Tyrannosaurus Rex but with the pace of Diplodocus.

'How did you get on?' Ed asked.

'4.53,' I replied, warily. 'How about yourself?'

'Second,' he answered matter-of-factly before handing me some biscuits to help me fill the emptiness I was now feeling inside. Reality 2, Ego 0. It had clearly been a day for star performances because the next person I spoke to was a gent called Rob Reynolds who'd just completed his first Half Ironman considerably faster than I managed my first (3–0) whereupon Joe appeared announcing that he'd won the 90–95-year-olds age-group so did I mind if we hung around for the awards ceremony (4–0).

All of this goes to show that, no matter how long I have been doing races, I am still poor enough to learn some valuable lessons, this one being that feeling your race has been a success does not depend on your athletic performance but instead on carefully selecting with whom you discuss your post-race results. My advice to all you triathletes and future multi-sporters out there is to lurk outside transition at bike collection time until you see some poor fly-caked sod limping in and then sidle up alongside them to jauntily ask, 'How did you get on?' as a way to force them, out of politeness, to ask how you did. This is a bit underhand, I know, but that's a matter for me, my conscience and, apparently, the National Security Association.

So, two races down and two to go, plus a training camp overseas to look forward to, and things continue to shape up nicely. My swimming is imperious, my cycling strong if not especially fast, and my running acceptable if you are happy to accept a cack-pants style that makes it look as though I've had some kind of stroke. Dave's training plan has made me fit, and my favourite pastime of nicking copper piping from building sites is an incredibly aerobic workout, which is paying handsome dividends. I have also blown away the winter cobwebs and reminded myself of some golden rules of transition – how to lay out your kit, how to make a quick exit on to the run as though you were legging it out of a curry house, and, crucially, how to make your results sound as good as you possibly can. This skill is not to be undervalued and forms an important part of the triathlete's armoury. Let me give you an example.

Since I started writing this book, I have become a British champion – twice! Earlier on I described how I had contrived to become National Masters 10-mile champion and, while taking a well-earned break from all this writing, I have also come first in my age group in the British Masters Athletics 10,000m Championships, bestowing upon me a gold medal and the title of National Masters Champion! Impressed? Well don't be, because not only was I the *first* in my age group to finish, I was also the *only* one in my age group to finish. What I did in that previous sentence was what all triathletes are notorious for doing after races, which is to make our results sound as good as they possibly can without telling an actual lie. In every triathlon, one person wins and the rest of us are left trying to make the best of it by coming out with cobblers like, 'I was in the top twenty in my age group' or 'I did a PB for the swim', each of which can be neatly summarised as 'I lost.' In every triathlon I've ever done, people cross the line and start wailing like Mariah Carey folding a theremin in half, coming out with justifications that wouldn't fool a hen, but which we need to share to un-bruise our egos.

It's fair to say that since I turned 40 I've profited from the availability of masters prizes and scarcity of masters competitors, and I now have so many medals that if I wore them all at once I'd need an osteopath to punch the crick out of my neck. One or two of these races have involved beating an actual person, but I've won a fair few by virtue of simply being alive. Don't get me wrong, being British Champion is a big deal for someone like me who has the social standing of a plughole and it's great to finally get a bit of recognition from someone other than the police. However, finishing first out of one does take some of the shine off my victory – as does the fact that I'll forever remember the race as the one where I was constantly hooking my shorts out of my bum crack. There's also the embarrassment that, despite concentrating really hard on my running form, I STILL looked crap on the photos, crossing the line with my mouth wide open like a basking shark preparing to swallow an acre of krill. By now you'll be well aware that when it comes to serious advice this book is about as useful as an episode of *Hong Kong Phooey*, and I don't generally make it my business to hand out tips to eager triathletes like a zookeeper feeding sprats to barking seals. However, to give you a bit of light relief from me crapping on about myself, I thought I'd try and pass on some examples so you can recognise triathlon tosh when you hear it.

| What We Say | What It Means |
| --- | --- |
| I finished in the top 20 in my age group | I finished 19th in my age group (out of twenty-three) and 347th overall |
| (For the over 50s) I finished second in my age group | There were two in my age group |
| Conditions were much harder than last year | I was slower than last year |
| I was 5th fastest on the bike | I am crap at running |

| | |
|---|---|
| I was third finisher from my club | I finished 347th overall |
| I've been struggling with a cold all week | I haven't trained hard enough |
| I overtook loads of people on the run | I didn't try hard enough on the bike |
| There are lots of ex-elites here racing as age-groupers and those in the armed forces are basically full-time athletes | I didn't qualify |
| If I'd been eighteen months older, I'd have finished in the top three in my age group | I also didn't qualify |
| I did a course PB | I've never raced here before |

Anyway, the important thing to remember is that I'm British champion. As yet, it doesn't seem to have made any difference to the way people treat me as I pound the pavements on my training runs and I still have to weave my way through the undulating blob monsters on their way to McDonalds. Don't these people know who I am? Why, at the Swashbucker Half Ironman I finished in the top twenty in my age group in a race full of ex-pros, despite having a cold all week, and if I'd been eighteen months older ...

# Chapter 8

When I am training for an Ironman there are certain clues that give that fact away:

1.  I attain a scrawny physique – doing Ironmans has made me look more haggard than ET's nutsack and my plummeting weight means I have to buy a whole new summer wardrobe, although, to be fair, the old one was full of restraining orders and photos of Kelly Brook. As an example, I vividly remember getting towards the end of the training programme I did for my very first Ironman in Canada and I was sitting in my friend Steve Hundal's back garden having just got back from a six-hour bike ride with him. By now I was so thin I could have got a tan by slotting my face into a toaster, and one of Steve's relations told me she thought I looked ill, whereupon Steve announced: 'That means you're ready!'

2.  I will generally cycle so many miles on my ride to work, with the wind blowing in my remaining hair, that the hush that descends over the office as I walk in isn't awe-inspired respect, it's my workmates holding their breath. And no wonder because my body odour can now bring down a camel at 50 paces. And this is despite

my washing machine being in permanent use trying to keep my kit clean. In fact, if the scientists in Cern want to see something that travels at a million miles an hour they should scrap the Large Hadron Collider and just come and watch my electricity meter.

3. Before I took up triathlon my entire diet could be summed up by the nursery rhyme 'One potato, two potato, three potato, four' and I was so fat I had man-boobs like a pair of toad skin saddlebags. I would sweat like soft cheese just getting out of a chair and I'd only manage to reach my holiday weight if that holiday took place on the planet Mercury. I still eat like this now, except that thanks to the extreme hunger caused by Ironman training I'll eat whatever is in the kitchen cupboard and frequently have post-ride meals with food combinations that would make Heston Blumenthal throw up.

4. Having spent years not realising that times like 4.30 a.m. actually existed, I can now be found slogging up and down my local pool while the general public are still coming in from the pub. It must be great to be an elite triathlete and train when you want, and I bet they don't have to sit through afternoon meetings at work with one eye open so it looks like they're awake, and the other closed because they were out running at five o'clock.

And all this is despite having an Ironman career that has been about as successful as a North Korean missile. As we shall see, despite the many Ironman races I have now done, I've got them right, I've got them wrong and I've got them badly, badly wrong.

I suppose it was inevitable that I would start doing Ironmans, although while I was training for my first one I was warned that the experience of a full-on Iron race would either make me love them, or never ever want to even hear the word Ironman again without assaulting the speaker. Having spent 2005 steadily improving in Olympic distance and Half Ironmans, I decided that 2006 would be the year to lose my Iron virginity by joining the aforementioned Steve Hundal, plus Steve Howes the Channel-swimming Iceman, to have a crack at Ironman Canada. It was a perfect choice for my first long-distance race because it was a country I had always wanted to visit to see if they really do shag mooses and pick up their own litter. It also meant that, having endured my training regime on top of my moody pre-Ironman nerves, Nicky would get a very nice holiday out of it. This mattered because I dread to think what patch of skin I would have lost if I'd said, 'Hey, we're off to Bolton.'

As usual I was biting off an awful lot more than I could chew by joining the Steves, because both of them were experienced athletes aiming to qualify for the Ironman World Championships in Hawaii. Steve Hundal is the most terrifyingly fast short-arse I have ever seen on a bike, while Steve Howes is a Barry Chuckle lookalike who has qualified for the Ironman World Championships in Hawaii so many times he has his own hula skirt – and he is a phenomenal athlete despite the double drawback of being both short AND ginger.

Training with the Steves involved following a punishing 12-week programme of steadily increasing hours and distances, culminating in a memorable day when I did a six-hour bike ride followed by a two-and-a-half hour run and a ten-hour lie-down in a dark room. Looking back at this time it was incredibly generous of the Steves to allow me to train with them when they were focusing on securing a world championship slot, although I didn't feel like expressing much gratitude at the time because I was so exhausted I'd finish every ride coughing like a chimney sweep in the advanced stages of black lung. One of the more memorable aspects of the Steves' training plan was called 'The Lung Run', a weekly two-hour, cross-country run around the badlands of South Warwickshire. They said it was aimed at building leg strength and giving us some mental toughness to call on when things got bad during the Ironman – gulp! This kind of run sounds benign but when I tell you that during its lifespan The Lung Run accounted for Steve Howes breaking a rib when he fell on a furrow that was frozen solid; Steve Hundal getting borderline hypothermia when he fell into a river that had burst its banks; and me getting ten stitches in my hand after ripping it open on barbed wire, then you'll get the picture that this was Ironman training the hard way.

Having survived this punishing regime I was certainly full of fitness immediately prior to the Canada race, if not confidence. On arriving at registration in the town of Penticton, which was playing host to the race, I was handed an awful lot of plastic bags to put my swim, bike, run and dry kit in, some stickers to plaster all over my bike, helmet and skin, and a programme with a photo of the fearsome Richter Pass. We would have to cross the pass during the bike leg and it looked like it should have Nepalese Sherpas manning the drinks station. I don't mind admitting I was a bag of nerves in the days leading up to the race. How Nicky didn't brain me with a track pump I'll never know. It was an enormous relief to all concerned when the race arrived and I could piss off out of everyone's way.

This was my first time swimming with this many people (over 2,000) but I didn't find the experience all that worrying, unlike Steve Howes who had gone down to the front with the piranha pack and received a kicking he'd never forget. Somehow I managed to come out of the water ahead of Steve Hundal, although he remedied that soon into the bike leg when he came past me (and 1,000 others!) like he had his arse on fire. The first 40 or so miles were slightly downhill before we turned north and Richter Pass reared up in front of us. Despite its fearsome reputation, I found myself doodling up it past toiling Yanks and reached the halfway point of the bike course well pleased. What follows is a section of the course known as 'The Six Bitches' in honour of the six rolling hills you encounter, which soften you up until you start to feel as though you are made of Play-Doh. This is followed by a climb called Yellow Lake, so-named because of all the dehydrated triathletes trying to wee in it. This climb was much harder than Richter and at about 80 miles into the 112 mile bike course I was starting to think that the world was my oyster, meaning there was a good chance it was going to make me vomit. I eventually rolled into transition after 6 hours 10 minutes and set about recalling the dire days of The Lung Run to give me something to 'call on.'

This worked a treat until exactly seventeen miles when a pain shot up the inside of my left leg, raced up my spine, rattled round my teeth and then raced back down to my leg again. I had cramp; not just the kind of cramp that makes you go 'Ow' but the sort that snaps you in half and leaves you rooted to the spot unable to move a single muscle. From where I stood I could see the 17 mile sign but I couldn't move, I couldn't speak and I couldn't even tell any appalling jokes. I began to have my first doubts about whether I could finish. Cramp, being evil, subsided after a time and I was able to walk, then jog, then run, then be rooted to the spot again cross-eyed with agony as another wave hit me at 21, 23, 25 and 26.1 miles. I managed to hobble over the finish line in 11 hours 48 minutes to the sound of a man with a microphone saying 'You are an Ironman!' It was a lovely feeling but secondary at that point to my search for any scrap of savoury food I could lay my teeth on – frankly after 12 hours of gels, fruit and sweets I'd have eaten the cardboard box that pizzas come in.

In the huge, thronging crowd it was ages before I found Nicky and the Steves, mostly because I'd given Nicky my glasses and without them the entire world looked like an episode of *Roobarb and Custard*. Nicky was quite emotional when she saw me, having known me from when I was a fleshy non-achiever. I also had a happy reunion with the Steves, who had finished either side of the 10-hour mark with Steve Howes securing his Hawaii slot agaaaaain, although with the amount of kit that I went and bought with the words 'IRONMAN FINISHER' emblazoned on it you'd have thought it was me off to Hawaii having won not only my age group but the entire race in a new world record.

It was next morning when I was nursing a bowl of cornflakes and a massive hangover at breakfast that the question about whether this was to be my only Ironman, or whether I would be condemned to a life of fruitless toil with absurdly large thigh muscles, was answered. Steve Howes spoke of possibly, maybe, perhaps doing Ironman Lake Placid the following year and without even waiting to be invited, or considering the financial implications, or the feelings of the somewhat furious-looking wife sat immediately to my left I said, 'I'm in.'

And so it was that about a week later, thanks to some secret Masonic back-door arrangement Steve had with the race organisers, I was an entrant in Ironman Lake Placid, this time with fellow Roth-er Mark Stewart, who had decided that he was pissed off knocking around with a 'Half Ironman UK' T-shirt and us all saying, 'The only trouble with that T-shirt is the word "half" on it.' In my defence, being an Ironman made me feel utterly invincible and, if you had put a bullet through my forehead the only difference it would have made is that I'd make a whistling noise when I ran. Evidence of this was the fact that just one day after returning from Canada I headed off to Rutland Water to take part in a Half Ironman called the Vitruvian.

After completing an Ironman this was surely going to be a piece of cake, and so it proved to be after an imperious swim and powerful first half of the bike course. In fact, all was going spiffingly until 25 miles into the bike course when I started getting a dull ache in my knee, which became a stabbing twinge and finally searing agony. It seems that in my lazy, arrogant haste to reassemble my bike after unpacking it from its bike box I had put my saddle back on too high and thus the repetitive overstretching with each pedal stroke had strained my knee, making me squeak like a rusty bog door. I arrived in transition with a leg that now resembled a chicken drumstick but, not to be deterred from finishing, set off on the run with a style that looked like I'd sat on my own testicles. As I limped along another triathlete of my acquaintance, who shall remain a nameless bastard, sidled past me and said, 'What's wrong?'

'Leg. Hurts,' I replied through gritted teeth.

'Ah, that old chestnut,' said Bastard before skipping lightly away.

And lo! I was sore distressed at this insult and accusation of malingering and the skies didst darken and there was a mighty clap of thunder as I didst chaseth after Bastard like a hellhound before I overtaketh him and chargeth all the way to the finish line in 1 hour and 16 minutes for 20 kilometres, where St John Ambulance didst give me painkillers, apply soothing creams, strappeth me up and calleth me a bloody idiot.

At least this medical tent experience teed me up nicely for my crack at Ironman Lake Placid a year later. Lake Placid is a beautiful spot in New York State famous for its Winter Olympics ski jumps and a giant man-eating crocodile that may or may not live in the lake, which was guaranteed to make the Ironman swim faintly unnerving. It's a race that is apparently usually held in either pouring rain or brain-cooking heat and in 2007 it proved to be the latter, which was good news for Nicky's tan and bad news for my prospects of finishing without looking like I'd been dragging a cartload of scrap metal through a housing estate. In the lead-up to the race I'd followed the same 12-week training programme as the year before when I did Ironman Canada, supplemented by my previously mentioned driving ban, which kicked in around this time and led to me doing so many miles on the bike I had to be intravenously fed orangeade and liquidised Monster Munch to keep me upright.

Once again, the swim proved to be my best bit of the race and I even managed to emerge just ahead of Mr Howes, although soon screwed that up by grabbing the wrong bag as I ran through transition and then had to battle against the incoming flow of Ironmen in a hurry to swap it for one that didn't have a pair of running shoes and a box of Jaffa Cakes in it. The bike course was a lot lumpier than Canada but, thanks to my enforced non-driving regime, I was round it in just over six hours before it was least-shit-foot forward for the run. Things were going okay until WHAM – the exact same cramp attack hit me in the exact same spot on my leg at the exact same distance as in Canada. As I stood stock-still, swearing mightily, Mark jogged past me looking genuinely concerned about whether or not I was going to live, let alone finish, but I bade him carry on or, if he could find a gun, shoot me in the head and put me out of my misery. As it was I got going again and managed to keep my pretty little legs moving to the finish line, which I reached in an underwhelming 11 hours and 53 minutes. I looked so gaunt that two medical attendants grabbed me, frog-marched me to the medical tent, shoved a drip in my arm and told me things like 'Way to goooo' and that I'd done a 'good jaaaaaab.'

I'd lost an absurd amount of weight during the race thanks to becoming massively dehydrated in the heat and it took several days of consuming lard and booze in New York with Nicky (her reward for having to listen to me re-live the race in the same kind of forensic detail reserved for crime reconstructions) before I was able to look like myself again and less like some kind of nightmarish Christmas decoration.

Not all my Ironman experiences have been bad and, by degrees, over the following years I started getting less inept at them. This may have been because I started being coached by Dave, who introduced a degree of competence into my pre-race planning, forcing me to consider such things as a pre-race eating plan, hydration strategy and not being a training dodger. The first Ironman Dave coached me for was Ironman Austria, which took place in Klagenfurt, a name guaranteed to get a snigger out of any schoolboy. With a beautiful swim in the blue waters of the Worther See and a cycle around the set of *The Sound of Music*, it's an event that attracts a lot of entrants, and one of the toughest parts of the race is getting registered before it sells out. My memories of this race are far more pleasant, with a swim of one hour on the nose followed by a bike leg of 5 hours 40 minutes and a somewhat shuffling but effective run to give me a much healthier-looking finishing time of 10 hours and 48 minutes – this despite it being so hot that Nicky was forced to remain in the beer tent for the duration of the marathon lest she run dangerously low on Holsten Pils. Being of Germanic extraction (one of my great-grandads snuck ashore in a WW1 U-boat), I felt much more at ease in Austria than I did in the US, and resolved to make more of the European triathlon scene. So I immediately booked to go and do Ironman Florida. Sigh.

My relative success in Austria led to a period of the strongest performances I have ever achieved. I ran my first sub-three-hour marathon without particularly focusing on any training for it, and was going so well on my bike that I rode off the front of the Coventry Road Club training group, earning me the affectionate nickname of 'Tosser'. All this was good news because, inspired by my steady ascent towards becoming a vaguely competent athlete, I had decided that at Ironman Florida I would set my sights on this being the place to secure my spot for the World Championships in the land of Magnum P.I. Joining me in Florida were Steve Howes (inevitably) and my great friend Phil Richmond, aka 'Tigger' due to his bouncy running style. Phil and I started doing triathlons at the same time and joined Coventry Triathletes in virtually the same week, sparking a close friendship that continues to this day despite him being unmasked as an Aston Villa supporter living in Coventry and having to move to Inverness for his own safety. This was going to be Phil's debut Ironman and he was looking forward to it enormously, not for the challenge but for the many opportunities it presented for faffing about with his kit, something at which Phil is world-class. Another man present was fellow Roth-attemptee Joe Reynolds, who had made himself even more exciting by deciding to do the race with a broken collarbone following his umpteenth bike crash.

In my previous North American races, I had become so dehydrated by the heat that I'd virtually turned into a pillar of salt, so this time I was determined to take steps to avoid the advanced stages of death by doing some acclimatisation. Finding places in the UK that are 30 degrees centigrade and 75 per cent humidity in October is not easy unless you count my mum's living room, but that's where Loughborough University Sports Science Service and their fiendish heat chamber came in. For a few weeks before the race I beat a lonely path from my home to Loughborough to sit on a turbo trainer in a small room packed full of heaters, humidifiers and wallpaper steamers, and pedal like mad for an hour while resident physiologist Beth Hanson analysed my heart rate, temperature, rate of fluid-loss and constant complaining. The acclimatization sessions were not only to get me used to racing in the heat, but were also designed to calculate how much I needed to drink during a race, when to drink and most importantly what to drink. This involved Beth maintaining a high degree of professionalism while taking blood and urine samples from an extremely sweaty and sweary man moaning about having a numb crotch. At the end of all this, I not only had an impressive array of sweat rashes but at last a tolerance for cycling in ovens. Nothing could stop me now!

A week before the race I went out on my final ride before packing my bike away. I was pedaling serenely, full of dreams of a sub-10 hour Ironman, when my thoughts were interrupted by an engine behind me. 'Hello,' I thought, 'that sounds a bit close I wonder if …' **BANG**. What happened next is a bit of a blur but I remember a terrific impact, everything turning upside down and then sliding gracefully down the road on my face before coming to a halt head first in a gutter. The only other thing I recall was the same engine revving frantically and then speeding off up the road. To cut a long story short, I was the victim of a hit and run incident that involved my back wheel, a blue Ford Transit and an utter bastard. The crash left me with a gashed face, skinned hips, multiple cuts and bruises, a sprained wrist and, more significantly, a fractured elbow and a shattered dream as I watched my Ironman go up in a puff of gravel. My stubborness and refusal to accept the blindingly obvious can occasionally serve me well. It did on this occasion because, despite my injuries and a bent bike, I got back on it, unwound the brakes to accommodate the bent back wheel, jammed it into a gear, clamped my hand on to the handlebars and pedalled home. Upon arriving I simply curled up on the settee and quietly fainted.

It wasn't until Nicky came in and took one look at my sheet-white, blood-caked face that I was whisked to hospital. Even now it's hard to put into words how I felt when the doctors told me my arm was broken. Even though I couldn't move it, even though they'd had to drain a syringe-full of blood from the joint to reduce the swelling, and even though I was so cross-eyed with pain

I thought the hospital was full of twins, I was clinging to the hope that I could still make the race. When they told me I'd be out of the game for six weeks at least, I did what any dignified, self-respecting adult would do – I cried. After a decent period of self-pity I reported the incident to the police. It might be a sign of my age, but the policeman who took my statement was so young I half expected him to write his report in alphabet spaghetti.

Unfortunately, without a registration number, which I didn't get due to having my face jammed into a kerb, we were down to studying CCTV of the area to see if a blue Transit popped up anywhere. We never found him, which was a great shame because the machine gun I'd hired for when we did ended up costing me a fortune. I decided to go to Florida anyway as the trip was paid for, and because it's not Coventry, so at least I got to spend some time lounging around in the sun drinking beer. The private apartment we stayed in was fantastic with a view over Panama City beach, and I'd have loved to have stayed there longer (and in less pain) although I did have to go to some lengths to hide the fact that I'd got blood and ooze all over the bathroom walls from changing my dressings while sat on the toilet. It was a bittersweet trip for me, with the genuine joy of seeing my friends, Phil especially, complete their Ironmans, combined with the depressing low of being left standing literally alone on the beach when the gun went and everyone started the race. I did my best to be cheerful, but mostly I was self-absorbed, miserable and a complete nightmare to be around. In fact, after my petulant, self-pitying display I'm surprised I've got any friends left. Watching races when you are injured is crap – even in a place as nice as Florida. I must admit, though, that I was genuinely overjoyed to see Phil bounce over the line to become an Ironman, and Steve Howes romp home in 9.57 – though at least now I suppose I could say that I got to a finish line before Steve.

Pain heals, girls like scars, and glory lasts for ever, so there was no possibility of me retreating into my shell or knocking Ironmans on the head. In fact, the first thing I did was to enter Ironman Florida for the following year – and I was going to finish that race come hell or fucking high water. The physical scars healed over the next few months although the mental ones took a bit longer to shake off, and I remember being so tense during my first cycling time trial of the following season that my neck muscles were locked up tighter than a male escort in Boy George's flat. Phil and coach Dave virtually had to prise my fingers off my handlebars with a claw hammer after the race. All of this did not bode particularly well for my return to Florida, although weighing more heavily on my mind and elbow was the prospect of completing ANOTHER Ironman first, this one called 'The Outlaw' and taking place on the sun-kissed shores of southern Nottingham. I'd entered this race before any of the Florida shenanigans happened, so was well and truly under pressure to sort my lily-liver out before the race came. Fortunately, Dave brushed over any mental weakness I may have been feeling by giving me a good, old-fashioned boot to the goolies (metaphorically speaking) in the form of a training plan that I'd need the energy levels of a crackhead to complete, along with a handy list of places where one could dispose of a van driver's body.

In the event, my subsequent performance at The Outlaw showed that it is Dave who knows best and not me. As a result of sticking to what he told me to do I smashed my Austria time to pieces, taking nearly half an hour off my personal best. This was the first year of The Outlaw race, although it's now a well-established fixture on the Iron calendar. Racing in Nottingham was much like racing in Austria except that the Austrians spoke much better English. My finishing time of 10 hours 24 minutes was not only a marvellous feeling but my finishing position inside the top thirty was a splendid novelty for me because, for once, the post-race recovery tent wasn't packed out with stinking, groaning men and women descending on the cake like a squadron of Japanese Zeroes.

The race had begun promisingly enough in the lake at Holme Pierrepoint and despite a 1,000-strong field of people all funnelling into the same three yards of water it was remarkably well-mannered compared to the punch-fests I've experienced elsewhere. Any odd clump about the head was forgotten by the time I hopped out of the water and tried to get my cloying wetsuit over my ankles, kicking my legs around like a drunk trying to shake a turd down his leg. My watch declared that I had done the swim in 56 minutes and 13 seconds, a huge PB that I almost blew by standing gaping slack-jawed at my watch for the next two minutes. The bike course was very fast with plenty to keep me occupied – people who didn't know how to ride a bloody bike mostly. There was one memorable moment when I realised that a wasp had perched on the arm of my sunglasses about 6 millimetres from my eyeball as I barrelled down the A6097 at 25mph.

Normally, when confronted with this kind of situation people react either by freezing on the spot and holding their breath, or they start waving their arms around like they are having a sword fight with the Invisible Man. I chose to stare it down, which gives you some sort of insight into what a dickhead I really am.

Mercifully I arrived back into transition unstung and set about tackling the run course, which took us to Nottingham City centre and back past Nottingham Forest's football ground. 'How times have changed,' I mused as I recalled the last time I ran along here was in the eighties and I was being chased by that load of Forest fans after Coventry had nicked an ill-deserved win there. The only other notable aspect of the run was that the last water and food station was manned by a load of girls from the nearby Hooters restaurant. It was perfect timing to have a load of stunning women turn up to serve my every whim just as I was caked in dead flies and my own snot. Let the records show that I did the bike in 5 hours 45 minutes and the run in 3 hours 35 and I did NOT try to touch up the Hooters girls your Honour.

Despite feeling buoyed by my return to form and my determination to avenge my lost Florida Ironman experience, things did not go well in the build-up to the second Florida trip. I had lost my carefully assembled Outlaw form almost immediately after the race. In my obligatory warm-up marathon, this time in Leicester, I was all set for another sub-three-hour finish until the twenty-first mile when the wheels came off in a massive way and I looked so pigeon-chested that people started chucking bread at me when I finally heaved myself home in 3.05. All in all not an ideal ego boost for what was supposed to be my next step towards the world stage of Ironmans with my first Hawaii qualification. And so it was that the best laid plans of mice and men often go astray, and the mouse ended up making a considerably better fist of things than I did.

Despite a final few weeks of training like I'd eaten a freezer full of Alberto Contador's contaminated beef, I ended up finishing over an hour slower than I managed at The Outlaw, which just goes to show that when you earnestly believe you can compensate for a lack of talent by doubling your efforts, there's no end to what you can't achieve. I couldn't blame the venue; I stayed in the same apartment I had stayed in the previous year (and I noticed they had changed the bathroom wallpaper). As ever the US crowd were fantastic – I find it hard to reconcile the charming, supportive and athletic people who race in and support Ironmans with a country where more than half the population are so fat they could clap out the theme tune to *Bonanza* on their man-boobs. No, my American cousins were not to blame for my failure, with the possible exception of one airport security guard at Panama City Beach who seemed to think that having a bike box and not being American qualified me for membership of the Taliban.

The weather was a tad cooler than it had been the previous year thanks to a nearby hurricane, thankfully downgraded to a mere tropical storm by race day. The choppiness of the waves didn't bother me at all as we struck out into the oily waters of BP's offshore drilling field and I was clinging to my PB hopes when I emerged back on to the beach exactly 59 minutes later. T1 was the usual melee of gels and smells and heading off on the bike I settled down for some long, flat roads. Unfortunately, you can add the word 'windy' to that list of descriptors and I soon found myself working harder than was strictly good for me. My growing tiredness and the fact that I never learn may account for why I then made a massive schoolboy error on the bike leg, which was to accept an energy drink from an outstretched arm at an aid station that I had never tried before. Energy drinks can be funny things and while one brand can turn you into a caped crusader, another can ensure you have a vomit-tastic time until you are purged of the poison. The rest of the bike leg was uneventful and I rolled into T2 with a bike time of just over five hours and 30 minutes, so still well on course to break the magic ten hour barrier. This wasn't how I was feeling though. I was conscious of feeling very tired, extremely light headed, and somewhat odd as I hunted through my bags for my socks and some kind of courage. After the obligatory first mile of shuffling I was soon into my stiff-legged stride and lasted until about mile ten of the marathon when I took a gel – and was lavishly sick all over the feet of the man who had handed it to me.

What followed was about the worst three hours of my life as I staggered along, doubled up with pain, throwing up about every twenty paces. It got so bad at one point that if I had died they'd have had to bury me in a bucket, and I was doing cartwheels trying to guess which end it was going to come out next. I never did get to the bottom of it, and whether it was the energy drink that made me sick or whether I had just overdone it on the bike, we shall never know. All I know is that having decided I'd rather suffer death before a 'DNF' (did not finish) I kept my legs and my bowels moving, milked the crowd for as much sympathy as I could get, and crossed the line with a bad stomach, bad headache and bad temper in a woeful 11 hours 48 minutes, just one minute faster than my debut Ironman in Canada and with a skid mark on my tri-suit that you couldn't remove with a fire. So a Hawaiian dream that began on such a high ended on a puke-strewn low and the prospect of a conversation with my coach Dave for which it was going to be advisable to wear brown trousers and a shirt the colour of blood. If I learned anything from this whole sorry episode it is:

1.  Do NOT try ANYTHING new on race day.

2.  Not all pain is gain.

3.  I need more bottle cages on my bike, although I draw the line at those ones that fit behind the saddle like a couple of rear rocket launchers.

4.  Drinking lemon scented bleach does not count towards your five portions of fruit a day.

5.  The secret to success is knowing who to blame for your failure.

I also learned that it is never, ever a good idea to go back to somewhere to race again, a lesson I have ruthlessly applied to every race I've ever done since. Except one …

# Chapter 9

Lost: one mojo. If found, please return to Martyn Brunt, under a duvet, Coventry. 'Lost mojo' is triathlon code for 'can't be bothered to train', which is something all triathletes go through from time to time. I suspect even she-who-is-Chrissie-Wellington has bouts of enthusiasm lower than the collective IQ rating of the average *Big Brother* house, and I had a right dose of it at the start of this season. My lost mojo could have been caused by any number of things:

1. It could have been be the arctic weather we experienced until March that kept my bike wheels in the clutches of my evil turbo trainer rather than sliding along the icy lanes like a penguin in a velvet wetsuit. I kept being invited by friends to go mountain biking in the snow but to me this kind of stupid thinking suggests they must be badly dehydrated.

2. It could have been contemplation of my advancing age. This is the year that I shuffled into the 45–49 age group, my back hurts, and the latest *Now That's What I Call Music* CD contains not one song I recognise. And it isn't even a CD. Welcome to middle age.

3.  It could be that I'm tired from doing too much cross-country running on courses that couldn't be harder if you had to do the water jumps while being kettled by the Egyptian riot police.

Generally I am a nightmare to be around when I'm in this sort of mood. I have all the personality of a VAT return, and gloomily pad around like a Dignitas tour guide. Consequently, I didn't see any of my friends for a while, let alone do any training with them, although it doesn't matter because the voices in my head keep me company. Plus, it's occasionally nice to have a break from them because it's very hard to keep up good after-dinner form while attending to dreary serfs who think *savoir faire* is a theme park near Warwick. When I'm in this frame of mind, the only time I ever cheer up is when I swim at 5.30 a.m. with my local swimming club. From 5.30 a.m. until 7.00 a.m. we have the pool to ourselves for carefree training, but at 7.00 a.m. this happy triathletes-only time comes to an end and the seething mass of sagging flesh otherwise known as 'the general public' is allowed in to stand pointedly at the end of the lanes willing us to get out so they can flop into the pool. I find there's nothing that puts a smile on my face like being chirpy with the sullen public at the precise moment they are at their most furious.

There are a number of solutions to hand whenever I am feeling like this:

1.  I can visit certain tax-cautious coffee shops for a massive jolt of caffeine, given that these days coffee is just a liquid fag equivalent.

2. I can try to get my hands on some performance-enhancing drugs by sending a round-robin email to all the crack addicts in a 30-mile radius.

3. I can try ending my annual 'no booze' New Year's resolution and start drinking again, although not to the point where I'm back to running through parks chasing ducks, shouting incoherent obscenities at passers-by and urinating freely through my trousers.

4. I can try eating less. As I've got older I've noticed I have acquired a craving for fish and chips, although even a small portion of chips from my local chippy is so large that if I ate them all I would die in the night. So on the basis that I don't have three stomachs like a cow, I have to make sure I eat no more than I can fit down my tri-shorts.

5. I can try varying my diet. In the past I have tried switching my diet away from pasta and jam sandwiches to more exciting foods, including one occasion when I switched to spicy chilli con carnes. My fiery breath lit up like an oil rig gas flare, melting my dentures, and it took three buckets of sand and the garden hose to put me out. I also once changed my usual breakfast of choice of strawberry jam sandwiches to my mate Phil's recipe for whisky porridge, which was a bit like having your brains smashed out by a slice of lemon wrapped around a large gold brick.

6. I can focus on preparing my bike for forthcoming races by taking it apart and cleaning it and screwing the bits together like a rubbish version of the hitman in *Day of the Jackal*.

7. I can go abroad. After all, I live in Coventry, and a quick glance out of the window confirms that any mentally capable person with access to transport wouldn't want to stick around.

If you're ever struggling with a lost mojo, never forget that 'impossible' is just a word – whereas 'fuck this for a game of soldiers' is a far more expressive seven words. It was for this reason I decided that, as part of my tortuous build-up to Challenge Roth, I would get outta this place and go on training camp to Lanzarote in a bid to freshen up my mood and my BO.

At the end of the last chapter I tried to inject a bit of mystery into proceedings by saying that I've successfully avoided returning to any scene of triumph or disaster with the exception of one place – and that place is Lanzarote, despite the fact that each time I go I swear that I will never, ever go back again. I've now been to the volcanic equivalent of Margate five times, twice of which were to do the infamous Ironman Lanzarote, which, as well as being billed as 'The Toughest Ironman in the World' remains the only Iron race I have ever done more than once – and bitterly, bitterly regretted it. The last time was just a couple of years ago and I crossed the line swearing (profusely) that not only was I never going to do that race again, but I was never going to set foot on that glorified pumice-stone of an island again in my life. It was the second time I'd finished there with a brand new personal-worst time and I was vehement that there was more chance of seeing Ryan Giggs on *Family Fortunes* than of seeing me in Lanzarote ever, ever again.

By now you may have reached the conclusion that I'm so full of crap I'm basically just a bowel with a haircut. So, true to my word as always, I returned to Lanzarote agaaaaiiinnn a few weeks before Roth to spend some happy hours labouring up hills into howling headwinds with a face like a buffalo straining to shit into a lake. In fairness to my worthless word-of-honour, at least I wasn't doing the Ironman there, having vowed never to return and having already parted with my not particularly hard-earned cash to do Roth. Instead, I was doing the Volcano Triathlon, an Olympic-distance race that follows part of the Ironman course – inevitably a hilly and windy part. The race takes place at a resort called Club La Santa, a sort of Stalag for athletes where the very fit gather to train, drink smoothies and compare physiques, a game I don't really indulge in thanks to having a body that looks like the last surviving semi-deflated balloon from a children's party. I'm only able to look like I have stomach muscles by shoving the plastic bit from the bottom of a Milk Tray box down my shirt. La Santa is a haven for all sorts of athletes, and those who just want to get fit in the sunshine by doing daily Body Kombat classes, which I popped in to, mainly to point out their tiresome misspelling of Combat, but also to find out what weapons were involved. I was very disappointed to learn that it's bare hands only, and the only body being 'kombatted' was my own, although I did have to agree with them that there is no room for guns in any public place, except perhaps the auditions for *The Apprentice*.

The Volcano is one of the main events of the year in Lanzarote, so me and three friends decided we'd give it a go and stay at La Santa for the whole week rather than try to mix it with the holidaymakers at Puerto del Carmen, who all looked about as healthy as the contents of an ashtray. Joining me on this trip were:

Neill Morgan – my good chum and a balding, Welsh primate who looks like a cross between Mitt Romney and a sexually ambiguous robot, and who glories in the nickname of 'Wetwipe' on account of his obsession with personal hygiene.

Andy Golden – a man whose sharp legal mind and athletic toughness is undermined by being ginger and having a voice like a bored carpet salesman. Andy runs his own firm of solicitors and spends most of his time staying in touch with how his clients are faring on his iPad, making the world beyond his screen just a dull blur.

Rich Palmer – a highly intelligent scientist and extremely strong cyclist whose constant urging for us to cycle faster when he rides with us is so delusional we have almost zapped him with lithium.

After a winter that made it feel like we'd spent six months on the ice planet Hoth, we arrived at Arricife and staggered off the plane into the Canarian sunshine with the giddy wonderment of newly freed battery hens, suitably refreshed after visiting the airport terminal bar (which is the only place you can drink at 6.00 a.m. without being judged). This feeling of well-being continued when we realised our apartment overlooked the venue for the outdoor aerobics classes, making our veranda a popular meeting point for middle-aged men pretending to be looking at the sunset. However, as anyone who's ever shared an apartment with three friends will know, it took about five minutes for the room to resemble a baboon prison, with kit and half-eaten grub all over the place and a toilet that made everyone who walked into it turn noisily blasphemous as they tried to warn others about the stink. In fact, my most vivid memory of the whole week is sitting on the veranda chair, which was positioned just outside the bathroom window, and weeping with laughter at the sound of Neill walking into the loo just after Andy had walked out, and subsequently retching like a fox with a pube stuck in its throat. Within five minutes of arriving the only things not strewn around the room were our valuables, which were secreted around the place depending on each owner's attitude to security. Andy hid his money in his pile of worn pants, while Neill kept his in his purse – or 'Essentials Case' as he insisted on calling it whenever anyone asked him, 'Why have you got a purse?'

The race took place just after our arrival at La Santa, meaning that the spectators were treated to some seemingly experienced triathletes hastily assembling their bikes in a flurry of spanners and bubble wrap before flailing around in transition unpacking kit and trying to remember how to lay it out. At the swim start, being an eighties football supporter, I went to the front of the bunch because it's the only place left where you can get a good, old-fashioned punch-up. I wasn't disappointed, getting a good mullering through the entire 22-minute swim – and just in case you missed that enormous hint, I'd like to just repeat that I did the swim in 22 minutes. The bike leg leaves La Santa, taking you to a town called Teguise and back with flat sections of the course that total about 8 yards, the rest comprising handlebar-chewing climbs, howling side-wind descents and a sand-blown sprint across Pothole Alley at Famara. I'd opted for a road bike with no tri-bars for the simple reason that I couldn't arsed to pack them, which is my excuse for why it took me 1 hour and 20 minutes to cover the 40k course. Once back at La Santa you head out on the running track before hitting the local roads down to the harbour and back. The 10k run was a much better 39 minutes despite it being hotter than Rich's now sunburnt neck.

In the battle of Apartment 149b, it was a resounding victory for me in a time of 2 hours 29 minutes finishing in sixty-ninth place overall and first in the 76–80 age group, which is a pity as I'm only 45. Next was Neill, who staggered over the finish line looking like an ageing Thundercat, followed by Andy who took time out from checking his iPad to dawdle over the line waving to his many female admirers and looking as sexy as a scabby knee. When you finish any race in Lanzarote, something special awaits you at the finish line, namely legendary race organiser Kenneth Gasque, the world's coolest man, who stays there to shake the hand of every finisher. I'd last shaken Kenneth's hand at the end of Ironman Lanzarote and on seeing me he said, 'Nice to see you back again,' with the same knowing grin as the clerk at my local magistrates court. Before I could say anything stupid about never coming back, the lads ushered me away and it's good to know that, no matter what I say, my friends always stand by me – although it's a bit unnerving when they do it in an otherwise deserted urinal.

After we got the race out of the way, the real reason why we were there revealed itself, which is that we were there to do miles on the bike. Lots and lots of miles on the bike. In the wind. Up hills. For hours and hours. Lanzarote is full of climbs that strike fear into the heart of any triathlete, and anyone who has ever done the Ironman there will know that they are pretty much ALL on the bike course. There's:

- Timanfaya (aka Fire Mountain), a long strip of steadily rising tarmac that stretches for miles in front of you as you grind up it, inevitably into a head wind.

- Haria, the longest climb on the island, which takes a bloody hour to get over, inevitably into a head wind.

- Mirador de Rio, shorter than the others with a spectacular view, but steeper and crueller because it takes you to the very edge of the island, not letting you turn one millimetre short, inevitably into a head wind.

- A climb whose name I don't know but which comes between Haria and Rio and is thus dubbed 'Pre Rio Rio'. Steeper than all the others, it is the only one on the Ironman course that I have seen people walking up – inevitably into a head wind.

If this weren't enough, there are several other leg-sapping stretches of road, all of which we tackled in a bid to shed a stone of flab and a long-term hangover. Over the seven days of our stay we did progressively longer rides, culminating in a 100-miler doing the whole Ironman course with the exception of the bit through the cellulite manufacturing capital of Puerto Del Carmen, full as it was of indolent British holidaymakers. This particular ride helped enormously to shake off my lost mojo, even though I bonked massively near the end and was found by the lads sat on a pavement outside a supermercado trying to give myself a Mars Bar enema.

The concept of being sat on a Canarian roadside feeling smashed is not a new one for me thanks to the two Ironmans I have done there. The first was back in 2008 when I entered in order to 'get it out of the way', having become fed up with people who saw me parading round in my Canada and Lake Placid T-shirts asking whether I'd done Lanzarote yet. And, like every triathlete, I constantly have something to prove (mostly that modern psychiatry doesn't work). I knew it was going to be hard because Iceman Howes had done it and told me that the bike course, inevitably into a head wind, will put at least one hour on your normal finishing time. Annoyingly, he was absolutely right; I crossed the line in 12 hours 45 minutes, vowing that this would be my one and only time at this race. Looking back at the photos from the race and seeing myself smiling, I wonder whether it was as hard as I remember, or whether I am just a grinning camera tart. I don't remember there being any particular episode of success or failure during the race – it was just a grind from start to finish with a bike leg that took me seven hours to complete and a run that I completed marginally faster than Nicky expected, hence her having to come legging it out of a bar she was drinking in to cheer me. Despite the unkind things I may have said about some of the holidaymakers in Puerto Del Carmen they were incredibly supportive of the athletes as we plodded down the 'beer mile' and the party atmosphere they create almost offsets the all-pervading smell of burgers that threatens to make you retch at every step. I remember one particular guy wearing a Coventry City shirt spotting the word 'Coventry' on my top as I ran past and drunkenly hurling his arms around me kissing me on the cheek, which would have been lovely if he hadn't used his tongue. All in all, it was 'job done' when I crossed the finish line and shook Kenneth's hand – so I thought …

The architect of my return was Neill, aka Wetwipe, who was doing the race himself in 2011 and who began a long, wearying campaign to get others to do it with him by bringing the subject up every five fucking minutes. Joe was the first to cave in, his resistance worn down by being of an age where he can sit on the train with his flies open and people assume it's absent-mindedness rather than a bold sexual gambit. Then I caved in, then Andy Golden and finally Tony Nutt, a once excellent athlete who has gone to seed and thus goes by the nickname of 'Prolapse'. Tony now spends so much time on golf courses that he could launch his own range of golf balls – and I think I can speak for many of my friends when I say that, at some point, we've all wanted to club Tony's balls. We were, of course, accompanied on this trip by the hubbly-bubbly coven of witchy gossips that comprise our wives, girlfriends and Joe's daughters, all attempting to get their five portions of fruit a day via the medium of pomegranate margaritas.

Having raced somewhat haphazardly in Lanzarote before, I chose my kit for this race with great care, designed to give me the best possible result and, more crucially, beat all my mates.

- My Kuota Kaliber time trial bike with deep-section Spinnergy wheels designed to eke out those few extra seconds when I'm not toiling into a head wind.

- A Giro aero helmet which was nicely aerodynamic but which is so tight on your head it leaves your ears feeling like a couple of braised lamb chops.

- A bento box fitted to my bike, which is ideal for storing energy gels where you can easily reach them and then squirt the contents all over your hands in comfort.

- An Ironman Lake Placid finisher's cap so that, no matter how bad you are looking, people will know you've done this sort of thing before.

- My Aquasphere goggles, which give you excellent visibility under water, although to be honest this is not always a good thing.

- Some large wrap-around sunglasses, perfect for seeing in very bright conditions and hiding large parts of your face when you are in pain.

Being a highly organised group, we contrived all to end up staying in completely different hotels, and I thought ours was fine until Nicky let me know different by writing the word 'knob' on my head in SPF50 sun cream while I slept on a pool lounger. We all managed to get together for meal times, though, all except Neill whose obsession with his hygiene meant that pre-race he would only eat in his own hotel, earning him the nickname of 'Bin Laden' for his refusal to leave his compound. On the drive to the race registration, which took place in a broom cupboard at Club La Santa, we noticed that most of the people out cycling appeared to be leaning at 45 degree angles thanks to the raking crosswinds. That made me wonder whether my selection of wheel was indeed worthy of the word tanned into my forehead.

Race day dawned with my watch alarm going off at 4.00 a.m. Pointless, really, because I'd been waking up every half an hour since midnight anyway. Setting the tone for the day ahead, I stepped out of bed and straight on to the inner-tube dust cap I'd lost the previous night, causing me to hop around the room in agony. Then came the attempt to force down a bit of breakfast, which always seems to be something of a trial before a race. Normally,

I have no problem wolfing down food at any hour of the day, but immediately before a race I struggle to swallow even a slice of toast unless I've chewed it about 50 times and then put it through a blender. As I was staying very close to the start line, it was just a short walk to the gallows, er, transition, where I stared fruitlessly at my bike for a while, bending over it pretending to make minor, but obviously crucial, technical adjustments, all in a bid to look much more professional than I actually was. Then it was wetsuit on, hat on, goggles on and a waddle into the water to stare into the distance in a manly fashion.

Remarkably, considering the beach was populated with 1,500 people all dressed in identical black rubber wetsuits with orange hats, I found Joe, Tony, Neill and Andy and wished them all just enough luck to ensure they finished behind me. There's an odd atmosphere at the start of any Ironman when 1,500 people are standing there with identical expressions that say, 'Oh, Christ, it's finally here,' but I didn't have time to ponder this for long because somewhere, a gun went off and 1,500 people all jumped on me. It's hard to describe a triathlon swim in any detail while still maintaining the rip-roaring pace of this book, so I'll just say the words 'sighting' (which is looking up to spot the course markers), 'scrappy', 'turn buoys' and 'gob full of salt water' and you'll get the picture. However, I emerged Kraken-like from the depths in 59 minutes feeling well pleased with myself ... for the final time that day.

Being a natural blond with baby soft skin, I am prone to getting sunburn if I stand for too long under a neon strip light. As such, the prospect of spending several hours with my lily-white shoulders exposed to the north African sun means I have to apply sun cream liberally or, better still, get someone else to apply it for me. In the transition tent at Lanzarote there were several people walking around with industrial sized bottles of sun block slapping it all over anyone who wanted it. I made it known to one of them that I needed basting, and she duly obliged. Unfortunately, what I hadn't realised was that my wetsuit had rubbed the skin under my arms during the swim, and as soon as the suncream touched the unseen red raw spots by my armpits I took off like a windmilling firework, scrabbling at my shoulders trying desperately to scrape the cream off.

Things did not improve on the bike and I realised I may have made a miscalculation in my choice of wheels when I was whizzing down the road to El Golfo and the crosswinds nearly blew me into the lava fields. The sheer effort and concentration required to stop myself going face first into a load of razor sharp rocks was beginning to get dispiriting and my progress got slower and slower as I tackled first Timanfaya and then Famara – although my spirits were raised briefly when I positively flew up the hill to Teguise leading me to shout, 'I am a CYCLIST!' before turning round at the roundabout into a howling gale. This proved how wind-assisted I had been, leading me to mumble, 'I am a FAILURE.' Then something happened that has never happened before or since – having reached the top of the mountain at Haria, I stopped my bike, climbed off and sat down beside the road. In all the Ironmans I've ever done, I have never stopped once, not even for a wee, preferring to carry out the foul deed while conducting the freewheel of shame and peeing down my leg. However, this was different because, even by comparison with being the victim of a hit-and-run a week before Ironman Florida, something happened in the run-up to this race that shattered my world so completely that I wasn't bothered if I never did another second's worth of triathlon in my life, and now was the time it chose to hit me.

Throughout this book I have talked at length (and hopefully with just the right amount of pride) about the various members of my family, but there's one member I haven't mentioned so far. She was born in 1963 with the then little-understood condition of Down's Syndrome, a chromosome defect that leaves people with mental and physical disabilities. This was a time when many disabled children went into homes or were not given opportunities to integrate into society, but she was taken home and brought up in a loving environment by parents who doted on her. Although they were warned by doctors that she would probably not live past the age of four, she defied the odds by learning to walk, then talk, then read, then write and a thousand other things. Though nothing at all was expected of her, she went to school, learned to paint and draw, play music, do her sums and charm absolutely everyone she met with a dazzling smile and cheeky laugh. Her name was Nichola (known as Nicky, though not to be confused with the other, more vocal Nicky Brunt to whom I am married) and she was my sister.

When I was born five years later, she adored me from the word go and we grew up as close as it's possible for a brother and sister to be. As I grew older, despite being her 'little' brother, I effectively became her big brother and protector, getting into more fights than I can remember with any kids who ever mocked her or stared at her for just a little too long. For her part, she started a job in a workshop and, while continuing to live at home with my parents, built a fulfilling and independent life for herself. Even when I left home, started a job, bought my own home, got married and so on, I went home to see her all the time to plague her when she was trying to watch telly, tease her about boys at work who had asked her out, and generally annoy her the way horrible little brothers are meant to do. When I took up triathlons she became my biggest fan and I would give her my finisher's medals to hang on her bedroom wall after taking them to work to show her friends what her brother had done. I can honestly say she never did a second's harm to anyone in her entire life – except when, in early 2011 at the age of 47, she died, and broke her little brother's heart.

It is hard to describe how I felt in the weeks after her death but 'numb' seems to be most appropriate. I remember that I didn't cry, because as painful as this was for me, it was infinitely more so for Mum who had now endured the double loss of my sister and my lovely dad, who had passed away nine months earlier at the age of 80. Someone had to deal with the million things that had to be dealt with, and that someone was going to be me, although I spent the next few weeks very much going through the motions when it came to life in general. In truth, I didn't want to go to Lanzarote, let alone do an Ironman there, because my mind was all over the place and I genuinely didn't give a toss about the race, or indeed anything. It may have been tiredness that finally brought the emotions to the surface, or it may have been the inevitable low spot you suffer during an Ironman, I don't know, but when I climbed off my bike at the top of Haria I could barely see through the tears that had suddenly welled up. I sat down on the side of the road and, I don't mind admitting, I cried my eyes out. After a decent period snivelling, I'd like to say that images of my sister urging me to carry on came into my head, but in truth I just got cold, deciding that I might as well ride down the other side of the mountain. Whether through catharsis or just warming up a bit, when I reached the bottom I was feeling much better and so carried on, not racing though, just pedalling and trying not to have any more self-pitying breakdowns. Although I was feeling better, I still wasn't feeling good, and cut an uninterested figure when Andy passed me and Neill rolled into transition just behind me. It took me 7 and a half hours to complete the bike course, and wearing an aero helmet for that amount of time leaves you with a headache that feels like you've tried to headbutt a comet.

Fortunately, the sight of my friends buzzing around me stirred my competitive soul and, on setting off on the run, it wasn't long before I steamrollered over the top of Andy. I was about halfway back on the first lap of the run when I saw Neill chugging towards me in the other direction.

'How far to the turn?' he yelled, with dreams of catching me burning in his eyes.

'Just round the corner,' I lied, hoping to make him inject some fruitless yet debilitating pace into his running, and loped off laughing. My jollity was short lived as I turned to complete the first of the three laps to hear that winner Timo Bracht had already finished and had done so in a new course record, making me feel distinctly inadequate and also making me want to grab hold of the announcer and pull his backside out through his nose. Further up the road I spied Neill trying to extricate himself from a roadside Portaloo while battling cramp.

'It was miles to the turn, you bastard,' said the Welsh one, which cheered me up enormously. Soon I also spotted Tony – walking – and ran alongside him to tell him I was on my last lap, news he greeted with a heartfelt 'Piss off.'

It's hard to describe the monotony of a marathon so again, through the medium of word association, I will merely say 'heat', 'gels' and 'burp' and once again you should get the picture. Finally, I saw the finishing chute and there, waiting at the end, was Kenneth Gasque, smiling like a benevolent assassin. I crossed the line in 13 hours and 10 minutes, a new personal worst by a margin that not even a handshake from Kenneth could assuage. At the finish, all I could manage was some tepid soup made of cardboard and boiled socks before shuffling out of transition, swearing on everything I hold sacred that I would never, NEVER, come to this bloody island again. Would I do this race again? The short answer is no. The long answer is nooooooooooooooooooooooo.

While I was waiting for Neill, Andy, Joe and Tony to finish (which they all did, and all behind me ha-ha-ha!) I got chatting to a fellow Brit called Dave Fenton, a fireman from Worcester, who had finished at the same time as me. As we stood and nattered about the ups and downs of our day, Dave revealed that a couple of years previously he'd had a skiing accident that nearly killed him and which left him partially paralysed. Doctors had given him fairly low odds of ever walking again – and here he was finishing his first Ironman, vowing to come back the following year to beat his time. Dave and I have subsequently become good friends, and I owe him a big one for telling me his story at that moment because it didn't half snap me out of my self-pity and made me realise that if my sister taught me one thing in life, it's that life is what you make it – so stop wallowing and get living. Despite a crap performance, I'd still bagged another Ironman finisher's medal and, on arriving back in the UK, almost the first thing I did was to go and visit my mum, hang the medal on my sister's bedroom wall, and quietly close the door behind me. Wherever you are sis, that one was for you.

# Chapter 10

Still with me? Well done you, you have the kind of tolerance for tedium that will make you the perfect Ironman. Although I write regularly in *220 Triathlon* magazine, it's always a genuine surprise to me that people read anything I have written because while Pushkin could write a classic like *The Captain's Daughter* in his second language, I can't even write a shopping list without putting a stray apostrophe in the word 'eggs'.

Before we plunge into the world of training for Ironmans and, more specifically, the looming black cloud of Challenge Roth, which is drifting inexorably towards us (me) like a bank of fog, we must talk about my international stardom.

'Must we?' you are no doubt thinking.

Yes, I'm afraid we must, because this may well be the only book I ever write and this is, therefore, my only chance to tell the world that I have represented Great Britain not once but FIVE times thanks to taking up triathlons. I have graced such events as the European Championships and World Finals a hatful of times – always assuming it is wee Jimmy Krankie's hat we're talking about. Be honest, if this were you writing this book and you had a chance to tell a somewhat captive audience about how you took on the world's finest athletes standing erect, swathed in a union flag and with ceremonial sword in hand shouting, 'Come and taste some British steel, foreign Johnnies,' then you'd probably try to find a way to shoehorn it in, too. Not that it is entirely irrelevant to the world of Ironmans because, as we shall see, the races I have taken part in are all 'Long Distance' championships and thus the experience between me bumbling along Iron-distance courses in my spotty Cov Tri skinsuit, and bumbling along them in my GB skinsuit, is a shared one. There are some differences between 'Long Course' and Ironman distances but I sense your boredom threshold is already being challenged and trying to point out the differences would be like a drunk priest trying to explain the immaculate conception on a broken Etch-a-Sketch.

Triathlon is one of those sports that gives you the opportunity to spend more time on foreign soil than Julian Assange, with plenty of chances to don the red-white-and-blue if you can meet the qualifying standard and have the same attitude towards accumulating massive debts as Fred Goodwin. They are not the cheapest affairs in the world, and once you've paid your race entry fee, booked your flights, sorted out your bike transportation, arranged your accommodation and purchased your kit (yes, purchased your own GB kit!) then you'll have just about enough left to buy a couple of flapjacks, or a semi-detached house in Nuneaton. I first became aware of racing for GB back in 2006 when, fresh from my new star-status as Ironman finisher, I went to the Belgian town of Brasschaat to take part in a middle-distance race known as the Superman Triathlon Vlaanderen – or 'zooperman' as the locals seemed to call it. Having thoroughly enjoyed it, a bunch of us, including the Steves, Tigger, Mark, Keith the Wookie, Joe (accompanied by an unspecified number of daughters), Tony No-Nutts and an Ali-Bongo style magician called Martin Burder, vowed to return the following year. We then learned that it was going to be used as the venue for the ETU European Championships, so if we wanted to race we'd have to qualify through our respective national bodies. This was England for most of us, the planet Tattooine for Keith and the Magic Circle for Martin. Fortunately the process for qualifying was fairly slipshod and involved us all submitting times for previous races over that distance. Every single one of us got in, although some of the results-fiddling made Robert Mugabe look like a rank amateur.

So it was that in 2007 I lined up in a GB skinsuit for the first time, sharing the moment with a bunch of good mates. It was a memorable debut and we all performed well, having been collectively warned by the team manager the night before that she'd 'heard about you Cov lot' and expressly forbidden from going out boozing, a lecture that would have carried more weight had it not been delivered in a bar she had just found us in. I remember my introduction to international racing being one of slight disbelief that here I was, last pick at school football and deemed *shit at sports* by old big-nosed Williams, representing my country and lining up against a bunch of overseas athletes be-decked in their national jerseys. The standard was much higher than I was used to from previous races but I gave a good account of myself, particularly on the run where I even overtook some elites (aka professionals), although in fairness they were about three laps ahead of me by the time I joined them on the run circuit. I have absolutely no idea who won the race but in the far more crucial Battle of the Friends, Steve Howes inevitably finished first, Mark was second, I was third, Magic Martin fourth, Tigger fifth and after that who gives a shit, although Nutty was definitely last.

This had definitely given me a taste for international athleticism so the following year I tried to pull the same stroke of buffing up my results and entering the ITU World Championships, which were being held at Almere in the Netherlands. And it was a proper world champs, too, unlike sports like snooker, which might as well be called the 'Britain and one bloke from China' championships. There were athletes there from Australia, Brazil, New Zealand, America and an absolute mob of Dutch, lining up against a GB team featuring such luminaries as me, Mark, Keith, Joe and Nutty. Being just a short hop across the Channel we decided to drive there – and when I say 'we' I mean that me and Keith shared a car. He drove while I slept, waking only to say, 'Let me know when we reach Calais and I'll take over' when we'd just passed a sign saying 'Wilkommen het Nederlands'. Joe had kindly agreed to let me sleep in one of the compartments in his big top family tent that was unoccupied by various of his daughters, so on arriving I spent a pleasant hour dozing and idly watching Keith trying gamely to stay awake while he pitched his tent in the dark, his sunken, bloodshot eyes lighting up the evening sky. Not that I had it completely free and easy chez Joe, though, because wherever I went in Billy Smart's big top I was forever being confronted with noisy daughters cackling or plotting a visit to a hash cake café behind their dad's back, or by Joe himself without his dentures. Joe's teeth are like stars – they come out at night.

If I thought the European Championships was a step up from what I was used to then the World Finals were the whole bloody staircase. These people were <u>serious</u> and had travelled halfway round the world to do this race, while I had snored there from Dover. So, despite having an ego the size of a planet, I was beginning to feel somewhat intimidated. Fortunately, things got off to a good start (for me) because the 4-kilometre swim was conducted in the roughest water I have ever been in. The swim was held in a massive inland lake and somewhere across the other side, far out of sight, a special someone had opened the sluice gates that regulate the lake's water levels. This led to the kind of waves racing across the lake that were last seen scaring Gene Hackman witless in *The Poseidon Adventure*. Hapless triathletes were being tempest tossed, unable to sight properly and getting extremely knackered battling the giant, deadly, killer waves. I, though, absolutely loved it. In my mind's eye, I cast a square-jawed, determined figure striking forth through the seething tide (although to the safety canoeists I probably looked like a flailing twat who kept going off course) and I was happy to emerge on to the wooden steps in one piece and waaaay ahead of some of the serious people.

The bike course was flat. Really flat. Flatter than most of the jokes in this book. It involved cycling along a flat, straight road for 15 miles, turning left at a windmill, cycling another 15 miles, tuning left at another windmill, cycling another 15 miles, turning left at a big pile of Delft and some other stereotypical Dutch items (actually it was another windmill) and then returning to the start to repeat the whole loop again. Nothing happened during the ride, precisely nothing. Some people overtook me, and I overtook some people. My crotch went numb from staying in the TT position for so long, and I longed for my back muscles to join it as they started to ache with the relentless pedalling. The trouble with flat courses is that there are no ups, and no downs, so no chance to get out of the saddle, vary your pace, freewheel or indeed do anything of note no matter how small. Had I known I would one day be writing about this in a book I'd have done something much more interesting, like drafted behind the race referee's bike or played a trombone with my backside. However, it was just a flat, monotonous ride that tested my patience, and now probably yours. On returning to transition, one of Joe's many daughters, Naomi, was doing her best to cause an international pile-up by leaning over the barrier wearing nought but a bikini with her assets on full show to the returning cyclists. The fact that she shouted my name as I went by made me a popular chap in T2 with the men of all nations who arrived at the same time as me, and who demanded to know her name and any advice I could provide on how they could ingratiate themselves with her.

On the subject of Joe, I was distinctly worried about him. Keith is as strong a swimmer as me so would have had no trouble with the waves. Nutty has also swum the Channel in a relay in the past, and although Mark isn't the strongest in the water he's not a man to let a moderate case of drowning slow him down. Joe, on the other hand, is an aquatic plodder not used to the kind of buffeting we had received. I'd kept a sharp lookout for signs of him on the bike course, or being paddled ashore while slumped across the front of a canoe. Now I was off on the run course and no sign of him. The mention of Naomi's bikini should indicate to you that it was now very, very hot and runners were flaking out all over the place. I kept plodding on and, despite a massive miscalculation of the distance I was supposed to run (namely that I thought it was two laps and not three so ran a second lap at a pace that mystified most of the people I was running with), I lumbered home in exactly eight hours, just ahead of two Americans, an Australian and the best athlete from the whole of Burkina Faso.

The elites had already finished long before us but the winner, a certain Chrissie Wellington, decided to wait at the finish line to personally congratulate every single GB finisher. Despite smelling like a fox's fart I got a kiss on the cheek while I bent low to kiss her hand, passing on my hereditary gingivitis. I just managed to burble something about my admiration for her achievements before having to go and lie down under a tree, where I stayed still for so long that I thought someone would come and draw a chalk outline around me. After a decent period of groaning, I went to the food area where Mark was attempting to eat his own weight (two and a half stone) in muffins and we discussed the likelihood of Joe's survival, before having a small wager on what part of the course we were likely to find his body on. The next person we saw was Keith, although sadly already in his civvies having been forced to pull out of the race due to feeling exhausted, possibly as a result of sleep deprivation. Joyously, the next person we saw was Joe, striding manfully over the finish line having defied the waves, the boredom, the heat, his ill-fitting teeth and having his daughters leered at by half the field. If anything, he looked quite baby-faced when he finished, by which I mean he was bald and angry looking.

Only Nutty was still somewhere out on the course, so we settled down to wait for the great man's arrival. Time ticked by and we were getting increasingly restless because the cut-off time was approaching, and Tone was cutting it ever more fine. With very few minutes left on the clock, the tannoy announcer informed the crowds there was one man still out there heading towards the finish and we should all give him a huge cheer when he arrived. We knew full well who this would be, so stood at the barriers and waited – and waited and waited. Eventually, Nutty hove into view over the horizon and it was all set up to be like a scene from a *Rocky* film with the bloodied but unbowed fighter stumbling forward to glory driven on by his sheer force of will. The music pounded, the crowds cheered and – with 500 metres to go – the cut-off time ticked over, they put a barrier across the finishing chute and told Tony to get his fat, dawdling arse off the course because they wanted to pack the barriers away. Yes, he'd gone and cocked it up by taking too long to complete his run, they'd applied the letter of the law and closed the course – no medal, no T-shirt and no Chrissy Kissy. Looking back it was very harsh to boot him off the course with just 500 metres to go. Very, very funny, but also harsh. For the rest of the stay in Almere, any time Tony did ANYTHING, such as peel a banana or put on his shoes, he had to endure us saying, 'Can you finish that, or do you need some more time?' He soon perked up by slinking off to Genk with Mark to stock up on Grimbergen. The only highlight on my journey home was trying to persuade the customs officers at Dover to search Joe's daughters for hash cake – which was the first time they shut up all bloody trip. More may have happened, but I don't know. I was asleep.

Because I am not a giant fruit machine that poops solid gold, I had a break from doing ITU races for Great Britain for a couple of years, allowing my bank statement to return to being printed in black ink, although Lloyds may just have run out of red. By 2011, my debt memories had faded and I decided I'd have another stab at international stardom by doing the European Long Distance Championships in Finland. During my absence from the world stage, British Triathlon had tightened up their qualifying procedures, no longer willing to take any chump with a pulse in order to make up the numbers but setting a qualifying standard designed to win actual medals. With my previous qualification method gone, I was fortunate to have one good result under my belt in the last 12 months – if I lied about the date on which the Outlaw Iron-race took place. Fortunately, my skulduggery paid off and it was a proud moment in the Brunt household when I received news of my selection with an e-mail from British Triathlon that effectively said, 'Give us £75 for your new skinsuit.'

Seriously, I had always wanted to travel to Finland and taste Moomin, and to finally do something of note in triathlon; racing for my country having actually been *selected* to do so, the first time I'd been picked for anything outside a police lineup. This was my first trip to Scandinavia and, even though the car park at Helsinki airport looked like it doubled as the outdoor set for Mordor, I really liked it. The race was in a lovely town called Tampere, home of the internationally renowned Spy Museum, which I can confirm is the best museum in the world, because I couldn't find it. Tampere was hosting the biggest championships in European Triathlon but the whole event was nicely low key, making a pleasant change after all the bellowing and Euro-disco you get with Ironmans. In fact, all I got for doing this race was a running cap and a helmet sticker that proved harder to get rid of than a treadmill fart.

Although I had donned the red-white-and-blue before, this was the first time I featured in a team of people chosen to do well, so I was distinctly nervous about being exposed as a talentless chancer among the country's top triathletes. It didn't help that I shared a transfer from the airport with Tom Sturdy, Britain's only elite in the race, but luckily he turned out to be a really nice person, as did almost everyone on the GB team. They all combined being serious about their racing with an avid interest in alcohol, particularly the comfortably talented Dave Hutchins who found the best bar in Tampere within an hour of our arrival. Preparations for the race were hampered slightly by sharing a hotel with a goth band and their entourage but with a couple of days in hand to walk around Tampere before the race, I promptly fell in love with the place. I'm not sure all the members of the GB team shared my view and some seemingly didn't emerge from the hotel except to race and shout at goths, but I was totally sold on the place to the extent that I was trying to swap my £75 skinsuit for a Finland kit – not that this stopped me from trying to beat all the athletes from a country better known for its rally drivers and herrings, mind you.

It was, perhaps, my sense of well-being that led to me having the best race of my life. Buoyed by feelings of tranquillity and goodwill to all Finns, I hurtled round the 4 kilometre swim course in a few seconds over 1 hour before seeking out my bike in the middle of the giant Ratina Athletics Stadium, an open-air transition that was basically a free pass for perverts to watch you getting changed. I breezed through T1 on a cloud of confidence and danced my way up the hill on my bike. Now, something I have learned over the years is that technology doesn't always make your life better. I first discovered this when I used one of those electrically controlled toilets on a train and, having pressed the button marked 'close', discovered that if you don't press the button marked 'lock' someone outside can push the button marked 'open', at which point the entire toilet wall slides away unveiling you to the rest of the carriage like a prize on a quiz show. Another example is my wireless bike computer, which has the sensor hidden in the wheel skewer – so well hidden, in fact, that the computer can never find the bloody signal. I've spent hours fiddling with the spoke magnet and fruitlessly spinning the front wheel while the speedometer stubbornly registers 0.0mph and my temper becomes more and more frayed.

On the bike leg in Tampere, my computer packed in 0.18 miles into the bike leg, leaving me to ride 75 miles on 'feel'. Asking a triathlete to judge how they're performing without the use of a gadget is a scenario about as likely as seeing George Michael and Vladimir Putin together on a tandem. Most annoying of all was that I'd wasted some of my weight allowance on the flight to Finland on the redundant computer, and as anyone who's ever taken a bike on a plane knows, milligrams count. One ounce over your limit and it's, *'That'll be an extra £150 and your soul for our lord Satan please sir.'*

Please forgive me a brief digression while we're on the subject of airlines because it's worth warning all you budding internationals out there that airlines are not noted for the warm welcome they give to people with bikes, and I reckon we're about nine months away from being forced to fly nude on a see-through plane. Then there's the food. Like most triathletes, I am mildly obsessive about food and dislike having my pre-race carbo-loading strategy disrupted by being served dinners that don't change even slightly from kitchen to toilet. I also dislike being charged £5 for a model of Ayers Rock masquerading as a steak and kidney pudding, thus having no money left to spend on daringly overpriced crisps. But don't dare to disrupt the stewardess' task of transferring hydrogenated fat into people's heads by asking for a healthy option, or they treat you like a shoe-bomber. Why this is such a big deal is beyond me. Say what you like but even the most fervent vegetarian nutter can't really do that much damage on a plane armed with a bushel of sage and a mystic aubergine. I won't name and shame the airline but it wasn't Finn Air, which I avoided because people keep disappearing into it.

Back in the race, I brushed off the absence of any ability to judge my pace with sang-froid or whatever its Finnish equivalent is, and just rode. In truth it wasn't the most scenic of bike courses, but riding on a closed motorway was certainly a novelty, if nothing else. And who needs scenery anyway? The race could have gone past Chichen Itza for all I know. All I saw was the tarmac three yards in front of my nose. Once again the standard of the field was high but my coach, Dave, had prepared me well and I rode in my usual steady way, albeit a slightly faster kind of steady than usual. Consequently I arrived back in T2 much sooner than I'd expected, and certainly much sooner than Nicky expected; I heard her mutter an audible 'Bloody hell!' when I came skipping lightly out on to the track for the start of the run. At this stage in any race I do, my unreasonably high expectations, coupled with a below par work ethic, usually result in an endless chain of crushing disappointments. But not this day, dear reader, for this day I floated on feet made of feathers, steadily picking my way through the field and making myself look less rubbish with every stride. This may be because of good, old-fashioned pride, and there's no doubt pulling on the international skinsuit makes you walk a little taller, if only because they make them a bit tight around your tackle. It may be because I was in Finland, land of the gods as far as I was concerned. Or it may be because I'd done what Dave said in his training plan for once. Either way, here I was starting a three-lap run through lovely Finnish parkland with my pants unsoiled and knees going in the direction I wanted them to. Once again, Nicky was heard to utter 'Bloody hell!' as

I strode past, although this might have been in response to the price of the beer. She said it again when I crossed the line in a new PB of 7:11.17. I didn't trouble the leaders, or even the chasers, but I lopped 50 minutes off my time at Almere and, in some very impressive company, I didn't look quite as crap as I could have. In fact, the only downer on the whole trip was after the flight home, trying to reclaim my bike from the carousel just as the flight from Benidorm landed, requiring me to lug my box through a bunch of people who looked like aggressive oven-ready turkeys and argue with some fish-faced old witch who tried to steal my trolley.

Buoyed by my new status as international man of mystery (as far as my non-tri friends who didn't know any better were concerned anyway) I then did something very, very stupid – I put my name forward for the ITU World Championships in Nevada later that year. This was stupid because:

1. It was in America where I always race badly.

2. I couldn't afford it.

3. It was the world championships and thus the standard would be even higher.

And

4. It was near Las Vegas where Nicky was keen to visit, stroll into a casino and take on the house at blackjack.

What could possibly go wrong? My main motivation for entering was that I wanted to get more than one race out of my GB skinsuit and make it feel a bit less like the most expensive piece of tri kit on earth, but there was another, unforeseen problem that made doing the race a stupid idea and rendered my skinsuit selection policy somewhat pointless ...

Think of Nevada, and what comes to mind? Baking sun, soaring temperatures and long, flat desert roads? Playing craps in Las Vegas while topless waitresses roller-skate through casinos serving you Cuba libre? Okay, that last one might be just me. I imagine you'd be surprised, then, if I told you that on my trip to Las Vegas for the ITU World Long Distance Championships, Nevada consisted of a cancelled swim, pouring rain, freezing temperatures, endlessly hilly roads, a streaming head-cold and crap of an entirely different kind. My preparations for the biggest triathlon of my life didn't get off to the best of starts when a week before the race I caught the only cold I'd had all year. I had to put up with seven days of snotty suffering, which allowed me to produce an impressive array of 'gold watches'. Things initially improved when I arrived at the Team GB hotel and a stirring Churchillian pre-race talk from team manager Tim Whitmarsh about the importance of beating Australians had me champing at the bit. However, torrential rain and the overnight temperature dropping to six degrees caused the ITU to declare it too cold for riding into the hills armed only with a wet skinsuit. On the morning of the race they cancelled the swim and ran the event as a bike/run. The concept of a swim being 'too cold' caused sharp words between teams from temperate and tropical countries, with the Canadians blaming the Americans, the New Zealanders blaming the Australians and, purely out of habit, the British blaming the French.

With the swim and mass-start punch-up gone, so were my chances of a good result and instead the race started as a time-trial with nationalities going off in groups. Alphabetically I was first man off in the GB 40–44 section and for two blissful minutes I was at the head of a phalanx of GB athletes storming up the road in Red Arrows formation. Then, teammate Dave Johnston worked out that I was going very, very slowly, at which point everybody buggered off up the road leaving me to ride alone, hacking up my innards like I was being exorcised. In many ways, the bike course was reminiscent of Ironman Lanzarote in that it was:

a) hilly,

b) windy, and

c) I was bloody awful.

Still, the scenery was lovely going through the desert and into the national park and it was nice to see old friends Roger Denton, Justin Littlechild, John Levick, Stuart Austin and half the field pass me, many of whom had time and breath to ask if I was all right as they whizzed by. I did manage to pass a few riders, including some Yanks who'd gone off too hard, some Japanese who were freezing to death and an Australian who was fat enough to smother a buffalo, but overall I was glad to arrive at T2 – which was actually T1 – and start shuffling. Despite feeling as comfortable as a woman at a Star Trek convention I started running surprisingly well and discovered that the only thing more satisfying than overtaking Americans is overtaking Americans who are walking.

At one point, I thought my running had been recognised by the crowds, who started cheering as I approached, at which point GB elite Rachel Joyce overtook me on her way to take victory and be crowned world champion, taking the applause and my dignity with her. I ran a fast final lap, mostly because I was being chased by a Canadian midget in alarming shorts, and it was with some relief that I crossed the finish line, collected my bike, caught the bus back to the hotel and went straight back to bed, all in one fluid movement. I had finished in 8 hours, 50 minutes slower than in Finland and so far down the field of finishers I could hear Tony Nutt laughing all the way from Britain. So it was that my attempt at world domination went the way of most evil geniuses and it was back to plan B with the Death Star.

Following my world-class world drubbing I wanted to head home with my tri-suit between my legs but no, oh no, no, no, Mrs B wanted to see the lights of Vegas and the sights of the Grand Canyon. I spent three days like a wet-lipped buffoon being frogmarched around casinos, watching my life's savings (£40) go up in a puff of cigar smoke. I even gave her the shirt off my back, which at least upset the Americans by revealing a back so hairy that if I ever leaned against flock wallpaper I'd have to be cut free. And no trip to Nevada would be complete without being driven out to Eagle Point in the SNOW to see the Grand Canyon, sneezing and freezing my balls off on the walk up to the edge of the canyon, which I couldn't look over because I'm scared of heights. Oh, take me back to Finland's plains and never let me roam again.

# Chapter 11

It is June, it is my final preparation race before Challenge Roth and AT LAST, after ten years of doing triathlons, I have FINALLY made it on to the podium at a race.

Actually that's not strictly true, I was on a podium waaaay back in 2004, but rather than standing on it I was slumped on it looking like a deflated testicle having just completed my first ever Half Ironman seven minutes inside the cut-off. The race was my very first attempt at any kind of longer-distance race and it took place in the hedgeless flatlands of Belgium. My abiding memory of it was shuffling past mirrored shop windows on run laps through a high street with my red face, sun-blocked mouth and spotty shirt making me look like a clown having a heart attack. The other thing I remember was that on the race photos, you can see that the winners' medal ceremony is GOING ON BEHIND ME while I'm still running! This humiliation led me to vow that one day I, too, would grace the podium. What I didn't realise was that that one day would come about 3,650 days later after a decade of basically turning up and farting out races with deeply average results.

The scene of my 2013 'triumph' was The Avenger Triathlon, a brand new middle-distance race held at Ragley Hall in Alcester. I'd set my sights on this race after finding out that one of the people helping to organise it was an old friend, Catherine O'Carroll, a woman who once conned me into running 15 miles to a lighthouse in

Majorca with the promise of a bus back, only to discover once there that there were no buses – ever! In fairness, she also conned some Germans into giving her a lift back, and then said, 'And my friend?' whereupon I sprang from the bush I'd been hiding in and flung myself up against the car window like a giant, sweaty Garfield.

I also fancied giving The Avenger a go because of the usual triathlete's reasons:

- Alcester is relatively local to the cut-price cack-hole that I live in, otherwise known as Coventry.

- There were a number of people I knew doing the race, including a bunch from my tri club, although, sadly, my old chum Tony Nutt had withdrawn after someone stole his tri-shorts off the washing line. I think it was the theft of the 12 pegs required to hold them up that really hurt him.

- The omens for success were good leading up to the race because I'd done three Half Ironmans already in the run-up to Roth and managed to crack them all out in under five hours, the most recent being the Cotswold 113 race, which I'd done just a week before and managed to take advantage of a notoriously fast course to record a new personal best of 4 hours 48 minutes.

- My friend Neill, Welsh Druid chieftain and sales consultant, used his mystical 'Dai Lama' powers of prediction to foretell that I would come second.

At least, that's what I thought he meant when he said, 'You're a loser.'

- It was a new race and thus good to support to help get it established on the triathlon calendar. And, with it being a new race, there was a chance the field of competitors wouldn't be as large as usual, giving me a much better chance of finishing higher up the leader board. This last one should henceforth be known as 'the real reason', because it is.

I'd also indulged in my very first aquathlon shortly before the Avenger and, while not exactly enjoying the experience, it gave me a much-needed reminder that longer-distance races are where it's at for me, because I sure ain't got the speed needed for the short ones. It seemed odd to be doing my first ever aquathlon after so long in the sport that my early results were written in Latin, and it's not exactly ideal preparation for 140.6 miles of toil but, to be honest, I'd been training hard and just fancied a bit of fun. An aquathlon, for the unenlightened, is a swim/run event that sits alongside duathlons as a sort of weird hybrid version of triathlon. I'm not sure why I had particularly avoided aquathlons up to this point, although I have consciously avoided duathlons, having done one at Ashbourne in the build-up to Ironman Canada. I entered under the pseudonym of 'Captain Pornoshorts' in honour of an infamous pair of lunchbox-revealing, electric blue tri-shorts I used to wear. The absence of the swim, the only bit I'm any good at, made it a miserable experience for me and meant that, on balance, I'd rather be locked in a flotation tank being pumped full of manure until I drown, than do another one.

At the aquathlon I also sort-of fancied my chances a bit given that I had been doing very well in the swim leg of every triathlon I'd done lately, having even led out of the water a couple of times, although the fact that I haven't gone on to win a single sodding race suggests I'm more Jan Sibberson than Chrissie Wellington. Again for you non-triathletes out there, Jan was an Ironman who won the swim leg of every race he did, setting world records in the process, but was then handed his beam-end in a high hat by the others on the bike and run. Like Jan, maybe I should market my own range of wetsuits, though in my case instead of 'Sailfish' they should be called 'Shitcyclist'. On top of my swimming form I'd also been running very well and added a second British title to my 2013 roll of dishonour, that of National Masters 10,000m track champion, with a performance that had even Mo Farah worried – worried that the credibility of his sport was being undermined by the fact that a title could be won by some shuffling twit who crossed the line sounding like an asthma clinic.

So, in my mind, the calculation went:

New age group + no cycling + swimming well + running well = medal.

Right? Er, wrong. What I hadn't considered was that with a 750m swim and 5k run the event would attract a lot of athletes who specialise in short, fast races as opposed to some gangling Ironman in training who's turned up on the off-chance. I realised things may not be about to go my way when I entered transition and saw that people seemed bemused by the presence of a pair of cacky old trainers that looked as though they'd been selected merely because the owner couldn't be bothered to swap the lock laces on to some better ones. Ahem. Things got worse when I set off in the swim where, instead of assuming my usual place at the front of the pack, I got pummelled and then left for dead by a massive shoal of sprinting piranhas. I came out of the water thoroughly chastened, huffed my way into the one and only transition and farted about putting socks on while everyone else donned their trainers and legged it up the road. Yes, that's right, I put socks on, and you may well be thinking 'tart' but the skin on my feet is smoother than an otter in a car wash and I wished to keep it that way. The 5k was fast and furious and I spent the entire run behind the same runner, inching closer with every one of my so-called strides. My target, however, wasn't about to let some lanky tosser come past and stayed ahead of me down the finishing straight, over the line, through the drinks station and over to the electronic results van. For my part I finished in 32:50 for thirty-sixth place blah-blah-blah who cares, I didn't win.

I finished feeling the same level of disappointment as when I realised Cape Town wasn't a place that is full of superheroes and, while the aquathlon was an interesting experience, it was too short to be of any real use for Ironman training. Furthermore, because there is no cycling, there is a distinct lack of opportunities to faff with your kit in transition – there's only so long you can stare at your trainers before you start to look like a simpleton.

I was much relieved, therefore, to return to my natural habitat of a longer-distance race at The Avenger, where not only did I have lots of opportunities to mess about with my kit but also to make some much-needed adjustments to my bike to make sure it was set up correctly for a hilly-ish course. In these financially straitened times I have taken to doing my own bike maintenance, as well as saving money by sourcing and producing my own race-day food through bin-scavenging, roadkill and good, old-fashioned thieving. I cut a noticeable figure in transition attending to my bike in my usual fashion, thumping away at the rear-mech because I always work on the basis that there is nothing on a bike that cannot be improved with a five pound lump hammer. While I was laying out my kit I went through my usual pre-race routine of looking skinny and trying to make sure all the people around me could see that I was wearing a T-shirt with the words 'Ironman Lanzarote' written in large letters on the front. You might feel that this comes across as a bit of hopeless posing in a bid to give myself some much-needed credibility and to intimidate those around me with my experience – and you'd be right. But don't be too judgemental about it, because it is what every single triathlete does, all the time, and the correct selection of race-day T-shirt is an important skill that must be finely tuned over many years.

Triathletes are a terrible bunch of posers really, which is surprising because what we've got going on isn't a particularly great look. When knocking about just before races or out among the general population, the 'look' for Ironman competitors tends to involve a sun visor hat of the style that lady golfers used to wear in the eighties, cycling sunglasses, a CoolMax T-shirt from the most appropriately impressive race you have ever done, knee length shorts, a pair of compression socks and open-toed sandals. Ideally, you will also be carrying a race-branded rucksack and sipping energy drink from an SIS bottle. The selection of T-shirt is vitally important and you need to practise to get it right. Turning up to a sprint-distance race wearing an Ironman Hawaii T-shirt, or wearing your GB kit for a local race, will make you look like a knob. You need to select a shirt that shows you have done a race harder than the one you are about to do, but not too much harder.

I realise that I'm making the world of triathlon sound like it's got more secret recognition symbols than Freemasonry, but that's only because it has. For example, if you haven't done a race harder than the one you are about to do then you should wear the best T-shirt you've got, although when it comes to 'best' there is a strict hierarchy of T-shirts that you must follow, starting with non-triathlon races at the bottom (running races, cycle sportives and the like) followed then by sprint-distance triathlons, then Olympic distance and so on though the distance ranks. However, a sprint triathlon T-shirt trumps a marathon T-shirt even though the latter is longer because any triathlon is deemed harder than a job, and everything trumps a Park Run T-shirt because triathletes assume the majority of Park Runners only do them on doctor's orders. There is, however, one absolutely golden rule which must be obeyed – no matter how unsuitable your chosen T-shirt is for the race you are about to do, it MUST be from a race you have actually done. Wearing a shirt you haven't earned is the greatest taboo in triathlon and being unmasked for claiming a false achievement is likely to see you driven out of town by a mob brandishing burning track pumps. The hierarchy of race T-shirts goes roughly thus:

| T shirt | What you think it says | What it really says |
|---|---|---|
| Any T-shirt from a 5k, 10k, or half marathon running race | I am a proper runner | I haven't done a triathlon |
| Finisher's T-shirt from a sprint triathlon | I am a triathlete | I am a novice |
| Marathon finisher's T-shirt | I am an endurance athlete | I am a crap cyclist |
| Finisher's T-shirt from an Olympic-distance triathlon | I am a better triathlete than anyone wearing a sprint triathlon T-shirt | I am either too old or too young to do anything longer than two and a half hours |
| Ironman 70.3/Middle distance finisher's T-shirt | I am a proper endurance athlete | I haven't done an Ironman |
| Something wacky or adventurous like Xterra, a Channel swim, or Land's End to John O'Groats bike ride | I am the real deal | I also haven't done an Ironman |
| Non-Ironman Ironman such as the Outlaw or, er, Challenge Roth | I have definitely done an Ironman | I still haven't done an Ironman |
| Ironman finisher's T-shirt | I AM AN IRONMAN!! | I haven't been to Hawaii |
| Double Ironman finisher's T-shirt | Ironman is for wimps | I've given up trying to get to Hawaii |
| Ironman Hawaii world championships finisher's T-shirt | Top this you bastards | This T-shirt cost me so much money I may have to fake my own death and move to Venezuela |

Resplendent as I was in bright yellow Ironman Lanzarote T-shirt I wasn't alone. For one thing just across the way I saw Dave Fenton, my fireman friend and the man who single-handedly got me back into triathlons after making me feel like a self-pitying goon, who was also wearing his Day-Glo Ironman Lanzarote T-shirt, making him look like a barrel-chested canary.

The swim in Ragley Hall's ornamental lake was in two waves – ladies, relays and men 45 and over in the first, men 44 and under in the second. Yours truly lined up in the old gimmers wave, going off first, I assume, because race organisers reckon we've been up half the night anyway going to the toilet. Entering the water at the start of a race is always a reflective moment because it is literally the point of no return. While on the bank you still have an opportunity to fake an injury or just slink away unseen from the crowds of identically dressed frogmen, but once you start to wade into the water, you are committed to the contest. No matter how cold the water feels; no matter what you put your foot on – or in – under the water; no matter whether your goggles leak or your swim cap rides up your head and makes you look like Papa Smurf, you have to keep going because there are people behind you queuing to follow you in. Backing out now would be something you would never, ever live down. Like every swim start, I was presented with a choice of slowly immersing myself under the water over the course of about a minute, letting the cold water seep into my wetsuit like the icy claw of death, or just simply plunging head first into the water and running the risk of having the breath knocked out of my body and ending up with a face more numb than Audley Harrison's. As usual I opted to stand waist deep for a few seconds until the cold water started to hit the small of my back and make me swear, then pitch forward quickly into the water and start windmilling furiously, shamed by all the people around me who have just dived in and are in danger of making me look like a coward.

I spent the usual, nervous pre-race minutes treading water while trying to pinch a metre or two over the start line without trying to look like I was. Then, as ever just at the moment when I was about to start my watch, the klaxon went and the cold, the leaky goggles and whatever I put my foot in were instantly forgotten as we headed off haphazardly towards the first buoy. At the first turn I realised to my horror that I was in the lead. Normally, you would think that this kind of endeavour would be a cause for celebration but it meant that, on a swim course I had never done before, with the entire wave behind me, all the pressure of potentially leading everyone the wrong way was on my shoulders. I was enormously relieved when a thump across my legs told me I was being overtaken and I could get on someone's feet and indulge in some massively irritating toe-tapping. The swim course was over two laps and, as we passed through the start area, we were close to the bank where I could see some people I knew standing watching me. The fact that they were not making any kind of encouraging gestures suggested I was flying, and you could almost see the expressions on their faces saying, 'He's going well, the wanker.' By now I knew there were at least a couple of swimmers in front of me that I could see, and there's always one stealthy type who has somehow snuck past on my blind side. I was convinced that one of the swimmers ahead of me was my mate and watery nemesis Keith, so I set about hammering it after his distinctive form, determined not to let him beat me out of the water and thus claim any bragging rights. I emerged from the water in fourth place behind two relay swimmers, neither of whom was Keith, and a woman/mermaid who must have done the 1900 metre swim in about 23 minutes flat. After chugging my way round transition, I was off on the 56-mile bike course, seeing Keith arriving out of the corner of my eye just as I was leaving – blimey, I had been quick!

Being a reasonable swimmer often means bike legs are a depressing procession of hearing the distant thwack-thwack-thwack of an approaching disc wheel as the bike monsters come past, but on this day it was me doing the overtaking as I passed the mermaid and one of the relay teams, and set about duelling with leading lady (and eventual female winner) Emillie Verroken. Emillie passed me after 22 miles of the course, and then passed me again after 28 miles, having gone off the wrong way, something which she seemed remarkably sanguine about when we briefly chatted as she nailed it past me. I was also to-ing and fro-ing with a relay cyclist and while I asserted my dominance on the climbs, he had more bottle than me on the descents, which led to a fairly even contest, helping me get round the first lap much quicker than I otherwise would have. By this time I had noticed the absence of anyone else from my wave overtaking me, particularly any men in the 45-plus age group, and I was trying to suppress excited thoughts about winning, mixed in with the usual ones about Holly Willoughby's dress. By now I had caught up with the back markers from the second wave who were on lap one, and there's nothing like powering past a bunch of slower riders to make you feel like a cycling god with quad muscles the width of the average human head. Mile 50 came and went and no one came past, then mile 55, at which point we turned and re-entered the grounds of Ragley Hall for the final mile of cycling. Then I heard it, thwack-thwack-thwack ... Yes, I'd finally been hunted down inside the last mile, and by my friend and all-round bike monster Greg Ashley, too.

Greg and I spent the dash through transition bickering about the poor sportsmanship of overtaking someone in the last mile of the bike course and he emerged on to the run 100 metres ahead – game on! The run was three laps of Ragley Hall's grasslands, which are about as flat as a taxi driver's man boob. If you ever visit the splendid grounds of Ragley Hall then be sure to have a look at the obelisk at the edge of the extensive woodland, and as you huff and puff your way up the hill to reach it, spare a thought that our run course went up there three strength-sapping times. Every yard of it was on the kind of lumpy grass you normally find in fields where cow pats live. Despite the terrain, by the end of lap one I'd closed the gap on Greg to about 20 metres, a cause of some surprise to the race commentator who said 'There goes Greg Ashley, one of the region's finest athletes, and ... oh?! That's, er, someone from Cov Tri behind him.'

Greg, however, is no mug, and I am. I had tried too hard, too soon to chase him down, and when he put a burst of pace in at the start of lap two, I had fewer answers than Wayne Rooney on *University Challenge*. Watching Greg steadily pull away and knowing I couldn't keep this pace up put me in an interesting position. As the gap soon became more like 500 metres, my chances of victory were gone unless my prayers for Greg's hamstrings to snap were answered, so I began to worry about hanging on to second. By now there were runners all over the course and it's hard work trying to figure out how old someone is when they all look like they've aged about twenty years since the start line. After spending the last lap pursued by paranoia and a squadron of flies, I finally crossed the line in second place for a silver medal and my first ever podium finish in a triathlon.

My face was the kind of colour you get from smoking sixty Lambert and Butler a day but I was still extremely happy, not only to have some virtual silverware to take home (actually it was a voucher) but also because this was the last stage of my Iron training for Challenge Roth. I could now look forward to that equally blissful and stressful period known as tapering. Greg was magnanimous in victory and said kind things about my futile attempts to catch him, and female winner Emillie was charming about me overtaking her less than 500 metres from the finish. I was neither magnanimous nor charming when I realised I'd beaten my old Worcester mate Dave by just 14 seconds – ha-ha-ha-ha!

So how does a silver medallist celebrate? Normally, what I most want at a finish line these days is a comfy chair and a colossal urn of tea. This time, however, I contented myself with a huge cardboard tub of breadcrumb-coated chicken parts and by heckling my slower clubmates as they toiled through Ragley's Matto Grosso. Keith came in for some especially rough treatment for losing to me in the swim.

And that was it – my training for Challenge Roth was done, and I'd finished it with my first ever triathlon medal, albeit with a not particularly impressive time of 5 hours 14 minutes. I was tired, and had the nagging feeling that I had done too many races, but I was obviously feeling strong enough over middle distances and had plenty of race practice under my belt. I was also now the holder of two British Masters running titles, a new Half Ironman PB and, best of all, a voucher for 10% off a training camp in France. Who says you can't earn a living at sport?

The final two weeks before any Iron race are spent 'tapering', which is training speak for not doing very much except the odd spin of the legs to make sure your muscles don't turn into a collection of reef knots. These days I just go for the odd gentle swim and jog with Freddie my springer spaniel. I avoid my bike after what happened to me in the lead-up to Ironman Florida – and not without good reason, either, because in the final few days before the race I still nearly came a cropper when I was cycling to work up a hill and a Range Rover overtook me, with the passenger emptying a Tesco carrier bag full of ice cubes in front of me. I know that my word is not exactly my bond but this is absolutely true, this really happened, and my immediate thoughts were:

a) Who the hell carries a bag full of ice cubes around with them?

b) Were they cold on his lap?

c) Why does the Range Rover cheapskate shop at Tesco?

What I should have thought was, 'What kind of arsehole sets out to deliberately hurt someone else and then run away?' I was more baffled than angry, especially because, as criminal masterminds go, the phantom ice cube dispenser wasn't exactly up there with Professor Moriarty. The ice cubes just bounced all over the tarmac leaving me a clear and untroubled enough path to have the confidence to remove both hands from the handlebars and make the Gareth Hunt Nescafé advert gesture (sorry for those of you too young to get this not-exactly topical reference, but look it up on YouTube and you'll see what I'm driving at). I'm well used to having a frank exchange of views with car drivers for whom a speed limit of 50 mph seems to represent the very minimum speed they should be driving at, and I find any disagreement I have with them over speeding, the use of mobile phones while driving and the non-existence of 'road tax' for cyclists is usually terminated with the use of a short phrase ending in 'off'. This isn't even the first time I've had stuff chucked at me out of car windows and in the past projectiles have included a bottle of Smirnoff Ice, a can of Carling Black Label and a glass, so with better timing the ice would have come in handy.

As I know to my cost, it pays to minimise risks in the final few days before your big race of the year, so I find it best to avoid the longer rides on my bike, and the main roads on my commute, instead just trying to lie still on the settee eating toast and annoying Nicky by leaving crumbs everywhere – although I'm not entirely sure if that counts as minimising risks!

# Chapter 12

So here we go then – the training is done, the warm-up racing is done, and the convoluted explanation of my accidental status has been laboured to death. We are now Deutschland bound!

Those of you who have received better educations will recall that there were four of us travelling down to Nuremberg for our own particular trial – me, Mark, Joe and Steve the Indian – and with the levels of organisation for which we have become notorious, we travelled at completely different times. In Steve's case, this made sense because he now lives in Brighton, while in my, Mark and Joe's case it was because we are useless at making plans, having once (genuinely) lost each other in a car park before a training ride. The plan was that Mark and I would travel down to Dover in Mark's enormous and fully gadgeted BMW with bikes laid lovingly in the back, while Joe and his wife Julie would travel separately in Joe's ever-reliable Volvo, with his bike slung on top of some daughters. Nicky and Mark's wife, Jane, sensibly opted to avoid travelling down to southern Germany taking up valuable bike space in a car that they would also have to share with two increasingly anxious and snappy pillocks. Instead they decided to leave the day before the race, flying to Munich where we would pick them up.

Mark spends so much time in Europe that he could never be adopted by anyone who votes UKIP. This made him the ideal travelling companion for a lazy tosser like me, content to sit back and let those who know what they are doing get on with it. Mark had sorted the travel arrangements for the Channel tunnel, our hotel in Nuremberg, our route through France and the Low Countries, an overnight stay along the way, an eclectic selection of music for his iPod (a bit too much eighties heavy metal for my liking but passengers can't be choosers) and a fantastic array of sweets. For my part, I brought my sunny disposition, a beginners guide to German and an iPod full of indie bands you have never heard of.

The *German For Beginners* guide I took was particularly important because wherever I go in the world, people always think I am German. I used to think this was just because of the lazy, stereotypical view Brits abroad have of Germans with blond hair, blue eyes and a slightly stern air about them. However, over the years I have been mistaken for being German by French, Poles, Danes, Yugoslavs and even the awful Dutch. This suggests there must be more to it, and even Germans seem to assume that I am German, which is slightly awkward because I don't speak any German at all, and have showed no aptitude for learning it after once getting 4 per cent in an exam at school. I have half-remembered a few German phrases from my one term at school, which I have successfully trotted out when approached by British timeshare salespeople on various Mediterranean islands on the assumption that they don't speak German either – and if they did they may wonder why, when asked if I speak any English, I have replied, 'Nein, der gummibaum ist im dem topf.' Roughly translated that means, 'No, the rubber tree is in the pot.'

Putting my kit together before the road trip south was the usual whirl of trying to remember everything I could possibly need. The weather in Bavaria was predicted to be sunny and warm, but I have been fooled by forecasts too many times to take any chances so, as well as all the usual items that I take to any long-distance race, I was also cramming my bag with unseasonal items such as arm warmers, base layers, rain jackets, track mitts and buffs. Basically there could have been a flood or an advancing glacier and I would have been ready for it. Despite going abroad for the best part of a week, the everyday clothes that I took could have fitted into my friend Neill's purse (sorry, I mean 'Essentials Case') and consisted of pants, socks, toothbrush, a selection of T-shirts from previous races and, just in case there was a pool at the hotel, a pair of 'small' Speedos that were so brief that I needed to visit a scrotal stylist before I could wear them in public.

My kit for Challenge Roth was as follows:

- Kuota Kredo bike that has 'Ironman World Champion' branded on the top tube. This, I presume, refers to someone other than me, unless you get called world champion for regularly finishing just inside the top 1,000.

- Spinnergy wheels purchased purely because they matched the colour of my bike, causing a massive row in the Brunt household and the revelation from my wife that her mother was right about me.

- Patriotic GB flag, nicked off a car during the Queen's Jubilee.

- Hastily purchased flip-flops to avoid a pre-swim barefoot walk across a gravel path and then stupidly worn for a toe-shredding 20-minute walk to bike racking.

- Ironman Lanzarote 2008 finisher's T-shirt, selected, of course, in a pathetic attempt to intimidate fellow competitors with my hardness and experience.

- A pair of England football shorts chosen with the specific intention of being confrontational but, in the event, only noticed by an Italian who laughed heartily.

- Brain-boiling sweat bucket, aka Giro aero helmet. One day I'll be a good enough triathlete to wear this without feeling like a knob.

- The latest shiny-thing-that-must-be-owned and which is not compatible with the many costly accessories of its former incarnations – aka bike computer.

- Great Britain skinsuit, mostly selected because my old Coventry Triathletes one was now so old that sections of it had gone see-through, providing anyone cycling behind me with an unwanted view all the way up my backside to the back of my teeth.

- A pair of sturdy running shoes (stuff lightness and speed, I want cushioning).

- A pair of compression socks. I have no idea whether these actually make any difference, but I got them as a free gift at a race – by which I mean I probably paid about £80 for them.

- Lucky pants.

- Cuddly toy, fondue set, radio alarm clock and a set of his and hers matching luggage.

Having squeezed all of this into Mark's car we bade our wives farewell, cranked up the Rush CD and headed for Dover. The journey passed quickly and, for two blokes off to do an Iron race, we were remarkably relaxed. Mark is a close friend and there's an old saying that states that, 'You should never trust a man who, when left alone in a room with a tea cosy, doesn't try it on.' I know that Mark, like myself, would put that tea cosy on his head in a flash. Incidents of note on the journey down included driving out of a motorway services with the roof box still open and our kit in danger of being spread halfway across Kent, and the obligatory humiliation of handing over my passport at the immigration kiosk and watching them stare uncomprehendingly at my face. I have lost a fair bit of weight since my passport photo was taken and my face is considerably thinner than it used to be. It now looks like my old face reflected in the back of a spoon. It is always disconcerting to watch the expressions of people at passport control trying to work out what age I am given that I don't so much look like I'm pushing 45 as dragging it. They clearly wonder what can possibly have happened to me to cause this transformation from a Miss Piggy lookalike into a scary Morrissey.

Once on the Continent the journey consisted of Mark buying something called a 'Travel Pussy' from a dispensing machine in a Belgian toilet that sat in the car window for the rest of the journey. Both of us were fascinated by the self-cleaning, revolving toilet seats in German motorway services, filming them on our phones to post on Facebook and also experimenting to see if we could stay sitting on them while they revolved. Soon our high jinks were at an end and reality began slowly to dawn as we rolled into the outskirts of Nuremberg. As I mentioned earlier, I had left Mark to book our hotel which was in the centre of the city just inside the old town walls. On the map, this looked like the perfect spot to stay, just a few miles away from the Race Headquarters in the small town of Roth, and handy to explore the city of Nuremberg itself, which I was keen to do.

As we drove up to the hotel doors I noticed a couple of bars opposite with blacked-out windows, coloured strips hanging from the doors and, lurking within, a couple of scantily clad ladies of advancing years or, as we in Britain call them, old slags. Yes, surprise surprise, Mark had booked us a hotel slap bang in the middle of Nuremberg's red light area. He protested his innocence, but the fact that he is a renowned perv meant none of us really believed him. As we were checking in, Joe arrived having done the journey in one go and subjected his family to sleeping in a lay-by en route rather than stopping at a hotel. Julie gave us both a warm welcome, pointedly ignored Joe and then went straight to the bar, while we broke the news to Joe's daughter that she was not likely to be the only one around this part of Nuremberg showing off her cleavage.

Having spent thirty minutes in my hotel room lovingly attending to my bike, I shoved a bit of deodorant up my armpits and also went to the bar, where Julie broke the news to us that the seedy bars opposite were only the starters. The main course was just around the corner where Nuremberg's biggest knocking-shop could be found. After two quick pints of Erdinger, Mark and I decided to go and have a shufty in the interests of scientific research. Now I like to think of myself as a cosmopolitan, experienced man of the world but I can honestly say this was the first time I had ever seen a half-a-mile-long, five-storey-high block of buildings with a semi-naked woman at every window, all calling me 'Shatsi' and beckoning me to engage them in conversation. As expected, our scrawny Ironman physiques and rabbit-in-headlights expressions attracted the attention of the many friendly ladies standing at their windows and we received numerous offers of sports massages, although they seemed to have a funny idea about where my hamstrings were. Being both married and British I spent most of the next five minutes staring at my shoes and mumbling, 'Nicht sprechen Deutsch,' as we walked past at the same speed I normally reserve for a five-kilometre run. We knew that our friends back at home would never believe us, so we spent a good deal of time trying to snatch a hurried photo through the windows of one of the sex-toy-covered walls before we were collared by some pimp and carried off wriggling into the darkness.

The next morning we drove to Munich to collect Nicky and Jane from the airport, and Nicky appeared at arrivals clutching a copy of *Fifty Shades of Grey* with a glint in her eye, which was all I needed. We then headed straight to race registration – at which point everything suddenly started becoming quite real. It was, as expected, superbly well organised and took place in a huge village full of stalls packed to the rafters with lovely carbon bikes, energy products and all sorts of weird and wonderful contraptions designed to make you a significantly better athlete for just a few thousand euros. Having entered the registration tent, signed a piece of paper that increasingly felt like my death warrant, and collected a wheelie bin full of instructions, timing chips, bike stickers, kitbags and race numbers, the next port of call was obviously the official Challenge Roth shop. It is very bad luck indeed to buy any item of clothing that has the race name on it before you have finished the race, and even worse form to wear it, but it's good to have a poke around and see if there is anything that you can buy with a clear conscience, so I opted for a bright red Roth towel and a pair of socks with the German flag on them, which should nicely confuse any timeshare sellers even more.

It was then back to the hotel for the favourite triathlete pastime of faffing, and I was able to pay forensic attention to all my kit, spreading it out on the bed and going through it piece by piece to make sure everything was in the correct bag, before unpacking it all and doing it again, then making up my energy drinks, putting the requisite

211

number of gels in my bike and run bags, applying stickers to everything and adding my numbers to my race belt – before unpacking it all yet again and starting over. Nicky wisely goes out whenever I am doing this because I become the world's most narky tit, and no matter how many times I do a big race I never, ever get any nicer to be around at this time. Once it is done, my mood improves slightly, but to watch me at these moments you'd think I was a scientist feverishly working on some new breakthrough for the benefit of all humanity instead of some middle-aged also ran about to do a race he's not going to win.

The day before the race was spent having a very slow wander around Nuremberg in search of bratwurst mit kartoffelsalat – not too far or too fast in case we tired our little legs out with all that arduous strolling – and racking our bikes. If registration was where the coming challenge felt real, the act of putting my beloved bike into the transition area was where it started to feel very, very real indeed. This is also the first time you are exposed to the full enormity of what you are about to do, with thousands of other athletes all racking their bikes at the same time as you, proving that this is not just some solitary occupation but one you are about to share with a legion of others. All of those others, of course, have been training as hard as you have, if not harder. Bike racking took place a few miles from Roth next to the Main Donnau canal and involved leaving my pride and joy in its allotted space, staring at it for five minutes as though I expected it suddenly to race off of its own accord, letting the tyres down a bit so they didn't expand in the heat and blow up, and then standing staring at my bike for another five minutes like I'd been hynotised by a boa constrictor. Once I had torn my gaze away from my bike, I began wandering around looking for where the entrance and exit were and counting the number of racks of bikes from the kit changing tent so I could find my bike when my ears were full of water and my mind full of dread. Roth has a split transition, which means that bikes and running kit are stored in different places, so it was then all back to Mark's car to drive back to Roth to leave my bag full of running clobber, stare at it like a village idiot, wander round looking for the run exit etc, etc.

Once all this was completed, it was time for the biggest dose of reality of all – the race briefing. This took place in a huge tent in the athletes' village, and was conducted in several languages at different times. The briefing in English was packed, mostly with Germans it has to be said, and it was where the race organisers highlight any information about the course that they think you should know, such as the right way to go, and the various crimes you can commit, which will result in punishments ranging from a two-minute penalty all the way up to being shot by firing squad. There are myriad different ways you can cop for a penalty in triathlons, including drafting (riding your bike in someone else's slipstream thus gaining an advantage by avoiding air resistance), littering, under-taking while cycling, riding on the wrong side of the road (British athletes take note!), verbally abusing marshals and not having the front of your tri suit zipped all the way up to the top, thus running the risk of inflaming the passions of spectators by showing them an inch of your bare chest. Phwoooar indeed!

It was at the race briefing that we finally bumped into Steve Mac, whose hotel was bloody miles away in the opposite direction to ours. Steve gave us his own briefing about his preparations for this race, all the training he had done and, specifically, how much he was looking forward to 'spanking' me, a clear indication he had spent too much time living in Brighton. Once the race briefing finished, I had the usual feeling of being a condemned man. The admin had all been done, my bike had been racked, I wasn't going to have time to do any more training and now we had been fully briefed, so we couldn't claim any kind of ignorance. The race was coming like the Cuban missile crisis, except it was not going to be averted.

All that was left to do now was to slink away with the thousands of others and try to get a decent night's sleep, which is easier said than done when you know what's coming in the morning. Firstly, there is the sense of impending doom to dog your sleeping steps, then there is the fact that you are full of food, having been carbo-loading for three days, and finally there is the fact that you are trying to get to sleep at about 7.00 p.m. while the rest of the world is out there living their everyday lives without knowing or giving a monkey's about what you are up to the next day. The good people of Nuremberg were going about their Saturday night business and saw no particular reason to do it any more quietly than normal. Dropping off to sleep while I could hear people laughing and joking in a foreign language was about as easy on my ears as Jedward singing 'Bohemian Rhapsody' – or indeed any song in the entire history of music. As I lay there listening to the sounds of happy people, I really, really envied them. They were not facing what I was facing, because they had the good sense not to put themselves in this stupid, stupid predicament. Eventually, I fell asleep somewhere between 9.00 p.m. and 10.00 p.m., 11.15 p.m., midnight, 2.00 a.m. and 3.15 a.m. I always sleep fitfully before a big race and this time was no different. There was nothing in particular waking me up except my own mind doing mental cartwheels, and each time I awoke and saw that it wasn't yet 4.00 a.m., I went back to sleep with a sense of enormous relief that my impending execution had been stayed. Until, of course, the moment when the clock flicked over to 4.00 a.m. and the alarm didn't go off – which didn't matter in the slightest as I'd been awake and staring at the thing since 3.35. Race day had arrived.

Getting up at 4.00 a.m. is like rising from the grave and is done just as silently. Nicky was also awake, getting up with me to travel to the race with Mark and Jane, so we vied for the bathroom with me getting first dibs for once on the grounds of how arsey I would be if I wasn't treated as the most important human being in the universe. Breakfast was a box of crushed cornflakes brought from home and some suspiciously watery milk purchased from a nearby delicatessen before I returned to the bathroom to try making a strenuous attempt to 'lighten the load' before we left, thus avoiding the horror of the race day Portaloos. This is, of course, futile because, as any triathlete knows, you only get the urge to go to the toilet once you have been fully zipped into your skinsuit and wetsuit. The car journey to the start was conducted in almost total silence with Nicky and Jane staying quiet, well used to what a pair of snapping turtles Mark and I both are on race day mornings, quite capable of starting an argument out of thin air. First light was just breaking at the transition area over 2,000 bikes and a dirty great canal.

By now tempers everywhere are fraying with the sound of bickering interspersed with nervous farting. We meet up with Joe and Julie and pose for some pre-race photos, mostly, I later learn, because we, and particularly I, look like a bunch of twats dressed up in track suit bottoms, slip on shoes, German flag socks and a beanie hat. We are then told to 'sod off and cheer up' by our wives and dispatched into transition to begin fiddling with our bikes. After pumping up my tyres and handing my track pump to a somewhat reluctant Nicky, I spot Mark running around trying to sort out a problem with his front tyre. Fortunately, bike mechanics are on hand, although queuing up for their attention as the clock is ticking down to your race start is about as enjoyable as having your pubes ripped out, knitted into a scarf and then wrapped around your neck to strangle you. Joe, meanwhile, is walking around in his usual state of semi-bewilderment, already clad in wetsuit and hat because his wave of swimmers is off before ours. I embark on the obligatory pre-race ritual of suddenly bursting for the loo as yesterday's bratwurst mit kartoffelsalat decides that it would like to leave me behind. I am left musing that the person at the ITU who insisted tri-suits should have zips at the back has never been a triathlete, because if they had been they'd know that trying to unzip yourself inside a European Portaloo that looks like it's been subjected to a dirty protest is about as easy as trying to carve a miniature crystal unicorn with your feet while sat on a bouncy castle.

Joe enters the water, turns to me, makes the sign of the cross and disappears into the murky deep. Mark is still running back and forth, so I wander over to where Nicky, Julia and Jane have stationed themselves on the canal bank to say a final ta-ta. Nicky has secured a good spot to watch us swim and come out of the water and is currently engaged in defending it with the same ferocity as the regiment at Rorke's Drift, shoving any would-be space invaders down the bank and almost into the water. This is a reminder, if ever I needed one, of why I married her. A big cannon goes bang and Joe's nightmare begins, while the next phalanx of swimmers is called up to the start line. The wave after that is mine, so it is time to cross the timing chip mat and enter the water. May the Lord have mercy upon my soul …

# Chapter 13

I am standing waist-deep in the waters of the Main Donnau Canal near Nuremberg in Germany. I am clad in a neoprene wetsuit, swim hat and goggles. Around me stand people dressed exactly the same as me – hundreds of them. Suddenly there is a loud bang, which is the start cannon for the wave in front of mine. There are so many swimmers in the canal that we are setting off in waves of a few hundred at a time – and mine is next. Some of us are standing near the edge on the sloping bank, others are bobbing about in the water, while yet others stay sitting on the bank silently listening to the power ballads being pumped out of the massive speakers attached to the bridge behind us.

When I can't put it off any longer, I glide into the water with all the grace of a windmilling bag of bones, select my starting position to keep the majority of the wave of swimmers on my right-hand side, kick the nearest Frenchman as hard as I can, fart about with my watch to make sure it is working and then lurk like a wallowing hippo waiting for the cannon's roar. Inevitably, my mind is wandering all over the place and I am trying manfully to get some kind of focus, repeating to myself 'Don't be so worried, you tart. This is the bit you like best. You've trained hard, raced well, and have avoided being mown down by a shithead in a van. You are here for your pleasure, so enjoy it!' Yeah, right!

## BOOM!

Schwimmen.

At the moment the cannon goes, all nerves and thoughts evaporate in an instant. All that matters now is getting my head down, my arms up, and getting one final dig at Jacques Cousteau. My normal swimming style is to breathe every two strokes and sight (look where I am going) every six so that I don't zigzag too far off course and swim into a bank or a boat, which I have seen done before and which made me laugh so much that I snorted sea water up my nose. As usual it is some time before I can settle into my favoured pattern because the first few hundred metres involve trying not to get booted in the face and wondering why everyone else except me seems to be unable to swim in a completely straight line. Consequently, I am sighting every two strokes instead of every six and trying to find a patch of clear water. Soon it comes as the people who have started off too fast fade and die and I surge forward like a scrawny version of *Free Willy*. Unfortunately, it isn't long before those of us at the front of the wave are swimming into the back of the wave in front of us, so we have to keep our wits about us to ensure we don't swim over the top of anyone – unless we were doing so on purpose because we are bastards, of course …

The swim is a single lap that heads up the canal for about a kilometre before reaching a turn buoy, then comes back the other way for two kilometres, around another buoy before an 800 metre dash for the exit. I know I am going well because I have swum through the wave in front, and the one in front of that, which contained Joe somewhere within its seething ranks. The fact that I have avoided getting into any bunches at all and haven't made any kind of contact with a single other swimmer makes me seriously think I am on for a PB, so when I round the second turn buoy I strike out for the swim exit like a man running up his drive to escape Jehovah's Witnesses. Exiting the water is never a graceful affair because you have just spent an hour lying down, and your sudden decision to get up causes all the blood to race out of your head and into your feet. I have never managed to look good coming out of a swim yet, and this is no exception as I clutch and claw at the carpeted slipway, trying desperately to get upright while looking even vaguely cool. As I run out of the water looking like a well-polished scrotum, I glance at my watch, which declares that I have completed 3.8 kilometres in 59 minutes, not a PB, but under the magic one-hour mark again and enough to make me grin like some kind of simpleton. The run through the changing tent is conducted with ruthless efficiency by everyone concerned except me as I spend five minutes flinging unwanted arm warmers and rain jackets all over the tent in search of gels to stuff in my pocket and my most precious possessions in the whole world, my pack of Jaffa Cakes. Then it's out into the big, wide world of the bike racks to retrieve my baby and head for the hills.

Fahrrad.

Everything has its downside, as the man said when his mother-in-law died but they came after him for the funeral expenses, and one of the downsides to me having a very good swim is that I am being passed by the stronger cyclists in the first few miles of the bike course. It always takes me a few miles to get going and the start of any Ironman cycle feels weird as you slowly dry out after your swim. I can only liken the vaguely grubby feeling you get as akin to travelling on an Inter-City coach. The bike course at Roth has a reputation for being fast, with few hills and lots of long, flat sections. Chrissie Wellington, who remains inexplicably popular despite how rubbish she made the rest of us look before she retired, made mincemeat of the course a few years ago, which helped to cement its status as one of the fastest bike rides on the Iron circuit. Of course any course is fast if you are good – and not if you are not ...

The Roth course is a two-lap affair through the Bavarian countryside and several Swiss-chocolate-box villages. Right from the word go, I find the route to be far lumpier than I was expecting. In previous Iron races I have always tried to have a good look round the bike course, even if it just means driving round in a car. This time, we hadn't bothered and, while the course isn't throwing up any major obstacles, I am growing disheartened quite soon into my ride, realising how slowly I am going and how many rolling hills there seem to be. I am now feeling really, really flat and not at all like I had in my warm-up races. I'm not particularly tired and nothing is hurting, I just don't seem to be able to get going at all. Luckily I have a number of differences between UK and German cycling to distract me:

1.  The German road surfaces are as smooth as silk.

2.  Every village has a loudspeaker playing power ballads.

3.   The crowds love you, which makes a nice change from being howled at by hostile, large people whose only physical achievement is exuding enough body heat to keep a chair warm.

The other thing that distracts me is anticipation of the famous Solarberg climb. It is not especially steep or long and the views from the top are not spectacular. What makes it so special is the MASSIVE crowd that gathers there and lines the road ten deep either side, leaving you a narrow tunnel to ride through. As I approach the foot of the climb, the crowds begin to thicken and the roadside barriers begin to get narrower. I see a solid wall of people ahead of me so prepare to swing right to follow the road round – only there is no road to the right, and I watch in genuine disbelief as the rider in front of me disappears into the smallest gap imaginable between two people in the throng. It is my go next and as I get nearer the gap opens and the crowd swallows me up. I am inside a tunnel of bellowing Germans clapping me on the back, throwing beer at me and screaming that I am 'Zooper Marteen'. This is honestly the most fun I have ever had on a bike and I grin my way up the climb, not quite believing what I am seeing.

I had heard about crowds at the Solarberg hill before the race, but nothing can prepare you for the sheer thrill of riding through a narrow tunnel of thousands of people cheering and sloshing Erdinger on you. The Solarberg comes near to the end of the lap and it gives me a much-needed kick up the backside, because I have been struggling up to this point. The effect on my speed is not instantaneous but I definitely start to pick up, although it still takes me over three hours to do the first 90k and my dreams of a sub-6-hour bike seem about as realistic as seeing Nigel Farage at the Eurovision Song Contest. I ride past Nicky, who is cheering me on at the halfway mark, and put on a temporary burst of speed to try to impress her – and just sort of keep it going. Having already been around the loop once I am conscious that I am having a much better time on the second lap, not least because I start to overtake people. Whether this is because I have sped up after a shocking first lap, or because they were slowing down, isn't clear. Either way, while not exactly ripping it up I am definitely shifting and feeling much better about it. Solarberg comes round a second time and the crowds are a bit thinner, many people clearly having wisely decided to go and watch the leaders who were now on the run rather than hang around plotting the physical decline of 2,000 also-rans. There are still plenty there to give me an Erdinger shampoo, though. About five miles from the end Mark comes whipping past me in a frenzied battle with some Italian, and then with less than a mile to go a cyclist comes inside me on a tight bend, overcooks the corner and rides straight into some hay bales at the side of the road. As he sprawls on the tarmac, I notice his name is 'Knut' – and who am I to argue?

Rolling in to transition, I notice that I have ridden the second 90k some 15 minutes faster than the first, for a 5:50 finish – not exactly earth-shattering stuff and down on my best times, but still under the six hour mark and respectable enough for a cycling bellend such as myself. I also notice that the cloudy, slightly breezy conditions we experienced throughout the ride have given way to sunshine and heat. It is now 2.00 p.m., the sun is high in the sky and it is about to make its presence felt. I wobble through transition on jelly legs, handing my bike to a stranger who I hope has something to do with race. Collecting my bag full of running kit and melted Jaffa Cakes, I settle down to make myself look more presentable, asking a glamorous helper named Heidi to slather me in factor 50 sun cream. I could have done it myself but at my age you have to take your kicks where you can get them. I've never seen the point of rushing helter-skelter through transitions in Ironmans. Sure, if you are Chris McCormack or Cameron Brown on your way to victory, then I can understand why you'd barely let your bum touch the chair, but for anyone who is arriving in the change tent at the same time as me, we're more off the pace than the Lib Dems, so grabbing a few extra seconds can't really do any harm. So it is, then, that I make sure I drink my drinks, eat my food, swap my socks for some lovely dry ones, do my laces up carefully and fall on my backside at a sensible pace before emerging blinking into the sunlight to begin the marathon.

Laufen.

Das shuffle would perhaps be a more fitting description than calling what follows 'running'. Nicky, Jane and Julie are waiting near the timing mat and I get a full volume shout of 'GO ON BRUNTY' from Nicky, which has my left ear ringing until the 21-kilometre mark. After an initial bit of running down some roads and through some woods the course takes us off down the wide, gravel towpaths of the Main Donnau canal. I start quite brightly, making good and steady progress over the first 10 kilometres, picking off runner after runner. In the dim distance I can see the familiar shape of Mark and his bolt upright running style but resolve to bide my time and reel him in gently rather than repeat the mistakes I had made in my warm-up races.

All is *wunderbar* until about the 20-kilometre point when, on a particularly long, straight and monotonous section of towpath, I start to feel pain. It doesn't seem to start in a particular place but radiates from my hamstrings until it encompasses the backs of both legs, my arse cheeks, my heels and my feet. I have no idea what is causing this because I haven't been going too hard, I've had my gels and energy drinks when I had planned to, and I haven't been anywhere near the naughty house of ill repute round the corner from the hotel. The pain isn't enough to stop me running, and it's nowhere near as bad as the cramp attacks I suffered in my early Ironmans, but it is just a wearying, sapping sort of pain that feels like I am being eaten from the toes up by a gummy crocodile. By 30k, my legs feel as though they have as much actual power as the two sidekicks who sit either side of Alan Sugar on *The Apprentice*. However, I keep myself moving with a vow that I have never walked in an Ironman, and I am not about to start now. Then I remember that I had to walk in my first Ironman in Canada and it takes as much willpower as I can muster not to say 'Sod this then' and just have a stroll for a while. I may as well have done because I was genuinely being matched for pace by some Dutch bloke who was power walking the whole course.

After 35 kilometres, I finally spot Steve Mac coming the other way as I head along the return leg of the towpath. He gives me a friendly shout and I reply by asking him to cook me a chicken bhuna, proving that, no matter how much pain I am in, I can always find time to wring the last drop out of an old joke. The pain by now is getting unbearable and I almost have a pretend toilet stop at one of the plastic toilet cubicles on the side of the course – 'pretend' because I don't need the toilet, I am just looking for an excuse to stop without obvious dishonour. However I remember a message I saw when I did Ironman Lake Placid that seemed appropriate and which helped me to pass by. In US races they encourage people to leave motivational messages written on big cards on the side of the road to help the athletes draw some inspiration. Most of them are just bollocks like 'Never let go of your dreams' and 'Chase the sun' but there was one, nailed to a tree, which said 'Pain is temporary – disgrace lasts forever' and I owe whoever wrote that a beer because it is a motto I have called on many times since.

With 5 kilometres to go, I enjoy another huge boost when I run into the market place in Roth. The run route takes us on a full lap of the square, which is lined with tables, all facing the runners, all full of very pissed Germans singing and shouting and waving beer glasses. Amidst all the cries of 'Zooper Marteeeen' I hear a familiar Cornish voice shout, 'You look terrible but keep going.' As I pass by a large, plate glass window I study my reflection and note that I am now covered in sweat, snot, dead flies and a semi-digested paste of melon and gels, with a face that looks like an angry, sunburned tortoise who has just stubbed his toe. All this makes me wonder whether the girls at the knocking shop would still want to rub my loins if they could see me now.

Abschließen.

As if Solar Hill, the Lände and Marktplatz Roth weren't enough, the finish line at Roth is brilliant beyond words, consisting of a big red square packed with literally thousands of cheering spectators. I don't know what it is about triathlons that appeals so much to spectators in Germany but they generate an atmosphere like no other place on earth and appear to absolutely love the sport, joining in the celebrations at every opportunity. Just like people do in Britain of course ... No matter how grim I was feeling two minutes before, the adrenaline rush is unbelievable and I fling my cap into the crowd, almost skipping across the line.

And there it was – race done. One minute I was just an ordinary bloke, while the next I was an ordinary bloke with a medal and a T-shirt. My finishing time in the end was 11 hours 15 minutes, well down on my best time but much better than my last performance in Lanzarote. To be honest, I felt neither happy nor sad about my time, I was just glad to get it done and keen to take steps to stop the pain that was pulsing through the lower half of my body. That said, I have never, ever experienced an atmosphere like the finish line at Roth. It was like winning the lottery, the Olympics and *The Price is Right* all rolled into one. I stood still for some minutes after I crossed the line just gaping in awe at the thousands of people cheering us all home. I wonder what the German is for 'gob-smacked'?

If I thought things at Challenge Roth couldn't get any better, I was much mistaken for two reasons:

1.  The recovery tent – after collecting my finisher's T-shirt (another one to be used for intimidatory purposes) I shuffled through to the area where the food is laid out, massages are provided, dry kitbags are stored and, if you are lucky, toilets are not foul and reeking. Usually, when I have finished a race like this I struggle to eat much and it is either soup or chocolate milkshake that I need to help restore me to the bosom of humanity. Often at finish lines you get neither, but at Roth I got both, plus a cup of tea, a pint of Erdinger and just about any foodstuff you can possibly imagine. It was like walking into Willy Wonka's chocolate factory. Even now I'm wondering if I dreamt it.

2.  The naked unisex shower tent – I know that Germany has a far less repressed attitude towards nudity than we do in Britain, but this was my first direct experience of it and it was a little difficult at first to take in that the changing tent was communal, that every man and woman in it was naked, and that absolutely no one could care less. The various shower rooms were separated between men and women, but aside from that it was do-as-you-please, although I think the organisers could be fairly sure that there was absolutely no one in the change tent who had the energy or flexibility to get up to anything sexually

untoward. It was a very liberating experience, although it took me ages to get Mark out of there.

Mark had finished ahead of me, which ensured I got a lift home, and we both emerged from the change tent to meet Nicky and Jane with distant smiles on our faces. We settled down at a bar near the finishing chute to watch people finishing and listen with wonder to the genuine hysteria of the crowd each time an athlete crossed the line. After 13 or so hours, India's number-one Steve came over the finish line and disappeared in search of a biriyani. A short time later, it went dark, the clock ticked over 14 hours and Joe emerged from the shadows to wend his way finishwards. We had all done it.

So that was it. I never did find out exactly what I should be called for finishing the race, but it didn't matter. Challenge Roth was a fantastic race and probably the most enjoyable one I had ever done. I will never forget the feeling I had while cycling up Solarberg as long as I live. As I sat drinking the pain away and boring the crap out of everyone with my minute-by-minute breakdown of the race (I wish I had written it all down, it might have made a better book), a huge fireworks display erupted overhead. Sitting drinking Erdinger and watching fireworks with Nicky and with our friends I came to the realisation that this was probably as good as it was ever going to get. I was never going to be an Ironman winner and, in all truth, I'm not sure I want to be looking at how the professionals have to live their lives to achieve success.

I saw a DVD many years ago called *What it Takes*, following the great Canadian Ironman World Champion

Peter Reid through a year of training and racing. Instead of inspiring me, it scared me witless looking at the sacrifices he was prepared to make. I was now in double figures for the number of Iron races I had done and my times had improved over the years, but never to the point where I was going to be in with a serious chance of qualifying for the world championships in Hawaii. The more I sat and thought about it, and what it would take to move up to the next level, the more I realised that I wasn't sure that's what I really wanted to do with my life. Bashing my head continually against this brick wall seemed less and less appealing. Suddenly, the thought of not doing any more, and doing shorter races for fun instead, didn't seem such heresy. I guess this was the point when I realised that Challenge Roth would be my last Ironman. I was tired, I was happy, I knew that it was never going to get any better than this and I'd only started this whole triathlon business by accident in the first place. I quietly informed Nicky of my decision, which delighted her to the point that she loudly informed everyone else of my decision there and then to make sure I couldn't go back on my word.

Of course, that raised the question of what I was going to do with my time now that it would not be devoted to the all-consuming Ironman training? Equally importantly was, how would I avoid ballooning back up to being a fat tub of lard once I'd consumed all the food I could get my hands on? More crucially still, it begged the question of how I would avoid getting dragged back in to the world of Ironmans when I have friends like Neill who appears to be some kind of paid agent in the employ of Ironman Lanzarote. I therefore resolved on the following:

- Stop buying crap - Triathletes are a salesman's dream because we buy things that are new whether we need them or not, and we will spend anything from a few quid on a new energy bar that tastes like a Glade PlugIn to thousands of quid on an endless pool that makes you look like a salmon trying to wriggle upstream to spawn. I am as guilty as anyone for buying overpriced junk such as a 'hydration system' which was basically just a plastic bag with a straw in it. From that moment on, I vowed I would not be paying one thin guilder for a carbon skinsuit or the latest piece of twat-dazzling technology for my wrist. The less stuff I buy, the less tempted I will be to use it.

- Stop buying race photos - Race photos generally make me look like a man as cheerful as Andy Murray in an Ingmar Bergman film. My only visible six-pack is on my forehead when I frown. Despite this, several of them adorn walls in my house. If I stop buying them, I will not be tempted to keep doing races in a bid to get some better ones or find that mythical creature – the photo I look good on.

- Stop looking at Facebook - Facebook is basically just a list of invitations to develop a gambling addiction and pictures of cats with fruit on their heads. It has, however, been a boon to triathletes wanting to bullshit about the amount of training they are doing with endless messages like 'Just done a great kettlebell class' or 'New Park Run PB this morning' and 'Nice 50-miler this morning despite the rain' that could be summarised by a single post saying 'I AM BETTER THAN YOU'. The net effect of these messages is to increase my guilt if I haven't been as far or as fast as other people's Facebook statuses allege, which leaves me with a choice of either trying to match these lies or just ignoring them and having another bun. From now on, I decided it would be buns all the way.

- Do shorter distances - So far I have existed largely as a Lidl-strength triathlete happy to climb hills on my bike at the speed of a Stannah stairlift. I know I shall never be a Brownlee but I seem to finish higher up the pecking order in shorter races – Half Ironmans particularly – than the full monty ones, so I decided that stepping down a distance and having some success would be a good way to ensure I am not drawn back to the underworld of 140.6 miles.

- Train for quality not quantity – this is something my coach Dave had drilled into me since he first saw that my idea of a training ride was 75 miles on my own without stopping, drinking, eating, or varying my pace by 0.1mph. My 'less is more' approach would mean stopping one of the 5.30 a.m.

swims that I do each week, which have dropped Nagasaki-like into my morning slumbers for the past eight years, and taking a more sedate approach to cycling to work through the school run.

- Lay off the booze - alcohol gives me super-powers such as approaching women in pubs and making toast at 3.00 a.m. On the downside, it seems to make me more argumentative and uncoordinated with a mild notion of invincibility, and has led to me logging on to the internet late at night and entering some stupid race or other in a fit of bravado. So from now on I would replace the value-brand lager that I normally enjoy outdoors, seated in an underpass with my dog, with things that are isotonic, hypotonic and hypertonic, which I did once know the difference between for about ten minutes.

Now that I have returned from Germany and set about the task of sticking to these promises, I have absolutely no idea how I will get on with them, or whether the absence of Ironmans in my life from now on will prove too difficult to cope with. However, whatever happens from now on, I'll always be an Ironman – even if I am just an accidental one.

# Epilogue

**2.00 a.m., November 2013**
I have just entered next year's Ironman Lanzarote. Oh,
well ☺